How to Conduct Productive Meetings

Strategies, Tips, and Tools to Ensure
Your Next Meeting Is Well Planned and Effective

ASTD
PRESS

Donald L. Kirkpatrick

ASTD Press is an internationally renowned source of insightful and practical information on workplace learning and performance topics, including training basics, evaluation and return-on-investment (ROI), instructional systems development (ISD), e-learning, leadership, and career development.

Ordering information: Books published by ASTD Press can be purchased by visiting our Website at store.astd.org or by calling 800.628.2783 or 703.683.8100.

Library of Congress Control Number: 2006923214

ISBN-10: 1-56286-453-X
ISBN-13: 978-1-56286-453-8

Manager, Acquisitions and Author Development: Mark Morrow
Copyeditor: April Davis
Indexer: April Davis
Interior Design and Production: Kathleen Schaner
Cover Design: Renita Wade
Cover Illustration: Todd Davidson

Printed by Victor Graphics, Inc., Baltimore, Maryland, www.victorgraphics.com.

Contents

Preface

I conducted conferences and workshops for the University of Wisconsin's Management Institute for over 25 years, and one of my favorite topics was time management. One of my regular questions to the participants was "What are your time robbers?" The three most frequently mentioned time robbers were waiting, unclear communication that resulted in rework, and time wasted in meetings. Participants responded with time wasted in meetings about 50 percent of the time!

The participants at these conferences and workshops were supervisors, foremen, and department heads who were referring primarily to staff meetings conducted by their bosses. From this, I regularly began conducting a workshop on how to conduct productive meetings.

It is interesting to note that I have seldom heard of training departments or corporate universities conducting workshops on this topic. They seem to be busy with programs on diversity, leadership, empowerment, teamwork, change management, and other popular topics. I have no quarrel with these topics, but I wonder what ever happened to meeting the need for productive meetings.

When Mark Morrow of ASTD asked me to write a book on the subject, I immediately agreed. My other new editions of *Evaluating Training Programs: The Four Levels* and *Improving Employee Performance Through Appraisal and Coaching* were finished, so I told Mark I was ready and eager to go.

This book is written for two audiences. First of all, it will be of practical help to those line managers who conduct departmental, project, and other types of meetings with subordinates. Next, it will be of practical help to training professionals who conduct workshops on the subject for line managers. (I also hope it will motivate them to do it!) It will also be a challenge to training professionals, regarding all of the training meetings they conduct. They know that participants expect the best from training professionals and don't want to waste any time in their meetings. Trainers may want to give each participant a copy of the book for further study and reference.

So, I urge you to accept the challenge of answering the pretest before you read the book. And be sure to do the posttest after reading the book to see what you learned or what concepts, principles, and techniques were confirmed.

I would personally like to thank April Michelle Davis for the excellent job of editing.

I wish to dedicate this book to my wife, Fern, for her patience and understanding of the time it takes to write a book.

Donald L. Kirkpatrick
dleekirk1@aol.com
July 2006

Pretest

What Do You Know About Productive Meetings?

Please complete the pretest before reading the book. Review each statement about meetings, and mark whether you agree or disagree.

Agree	Disagree		
☐	☐	1.	A meeting is the best way to communicate information to a group of people.
☐	☐	2.	A meeting is the best way to get information from several people.
☐	☐	3.	A meeting is necessary when there is a problem to solve.
☐	☐	4.	A meeting is the best way to train and develop people.
☐	☐	5.	A meeting is productive if the leader's objectives are accomplished.
☐	☐	6.	A meeting is productive if the leader's objectives are accomplished in a minimum amount of time.
☐	☐	7.	A meeting is productive if the leader's objectives are accomplished in a minimum amount of time with satisfied participants.
☐	☐	8.	The cost of a meeting can usually be accurately determined.
☐	☐	9.	The benefits of a meeting can usually be accurately determined.
☐	☐	10.	One of the most costly aspects of nonproductive meetings can be the negative attitudes on the part of those attending.
☐	☐	11.	Most of the causes of nonproductive meetings are under the control of the leader.
☐	☐	12.	Bad scheduling can result in nonproductive meetings.

Agree	Disagree	
☐	☐	13. Poor facilities can contribute to nonproductive meetings.
☐	☐	14. A meeting leader is more effective as a catalyst than a strong leader.
☐	☐	15. To have a productive meeting, all or nearly all of the participants must take an active part.
☐	☐	16. Time scheduling is important to a meeting's success.
☐	☐	17. Physical facilities are important to the success of the meeting.
☐	☐	18. An important part of preparation is to be sure that the right people are attending.
☐	☐	19. A flipchart, overhead projector, Microsoft PowerPoint, or other audiovisual aid should be standard equipment for every meeting.
☐	☐	20. If the leader has properly planned for physical facilities and audiovisual aids, there is no reason to check on them prior to the meeting.
☐	☐	21. Proper advance notice to participants is important for productive meetings.
☐	☐	22. Microsoft PowerPoint is more effective than using aids such as the flipchart and overhead projector.
☐	☐	23. The shorter a presentation, the more effective it is.
☐	☐	24. Humor always improves the effectiveness of a presentation.
☐	☐	25. The Kirkpatrick PIE (practical, interactive, and enjoyable) approach should be used by all meeting leaders.
☐	☐	26. If a participant asks a question, it should be answered in the meeting.
☐	☐	27. Overhead questions should be used more frequently than direct questions.
☐	☐	28. A question-and-answer period is a good way to end a meeting.
☐	☐	29. The amount of enthusiasm by participants is directly related to their participation.
☐	☐	30. Fear of being embarrassed or ridiculed by the leader is a frequent cause of nonparticipation and lack of enthusiasm.
☐	☐	31. Enthusiasm on the part of the leader begets enthusiasm.

Agree	Disagree	
☐	☐	32. Participants should leave the meeting thinking, "I'm glad I came!"
☐	☐	33. A leader should start the meeting on time even if some of the participants aren't there.
☐	☐	34. The introductory part of a meeting should get the attention of the participants and clarify meeting objectives.
☐	☐	35. It is easier to get participation than to control a meeting.
☐	☐	36. The best way to control a meeting is to prevent it from getting out of control.
☐	☐	37. If a participant is causing problems, the leader should handle the situation without embarrassing or ridiculing the participant.
☐	☐	38. A leader should always maintain self-control in a meeting.
☐	☐	39. When introducing a speaker, the chairperson should remember that the shorter the introduction the better.
☐	☐	40. When making a presentation, the presenter is more effective when using Microsoft PowerPoint than overhead transparencies.
☐	☐	41. It's the responsibility of the chairperson, not the speaker, to be sure the meeting runs on schedule.
☐	☐	42. A leader can always tell whether the meeting has been productive.
☐	☐	43. Participants can always tell whether the meeting has been productive.
☐	☐	44. A trained observer can always tell whether the meeting has been productive.
☐	☐	45. An instructor should use the leader, participants, and trained observer to determine whether the meeting has been productive.
☐	☐	46. The objective of instructor-led meetings is to increase knowledge, increase skills, and/or change attitudes.
☐	☐	47. The most important factor in instructor-led meetings is the effectiveness of the leader.
☐	☐	48. Trainers from within the organization are more effective than outside consultants.

Agree	Disagree	
☐	☐	49. In instructor-led meetings, the more participation the better.
☐	☐	50. The words *trainer* and *facilitator* have the same meaning.
☐	☐	51. In-house training programs are more effective than e-learning training programs.
☐	☐	52. Instructor-led programs are more effective than e-learning training programs.
☐	☐	53. The best approach to training participants is blended learning, which combines e-learning with instructor-led programs.
☐	☐	54. Trainers should conduct a workshop for managers on how to conduct productive meetings.
☐	☐	55. If trainers don't initiate it, managers should ask trainers to conduct a workshop on how to conduct productive meetings.

Chapter 1

How to Determine When a Meeting is Necessary and Productive

When Is a Meeting Necessary?

The word *necessary* is probably too strong. A meeting is never absolutely necessary. Life would go on and organizations would continue to operate even if meetings were not held. Substitute approaches could be made. The substitute approaches might cost more or be less effective, but they could be used.

The word *desirable* is a better word.

Consider the different types of meetings, and see whether the meeting or another approach is desirable. In making this decision, consider alternative approaches to accomplish the objectives.

Information-Giving Meeting

Before deciding to have a meeting to give information, the leader should consider the alternatives, such as a written memo or report. Obviously, the written approach would be cheaper, but the question is *Would people understand the message as well?* If the leader feels that the information would not be understood (and perhaps not even be read), a meeting might be desirable (even though more expensive) to call the people together and present the information orally. Also, visual aids could be used to maintain interest and help create understanding.

Sometimes a meeting is called to create proper attitudes or, more specifically, to sell the participants on an

Do—
Review corporate progress, particularly in a multidivisional company, and state clearly the divisional goals.

1

idea, policy, or decision that has been made. It is more than an information-giving meeting. When a leader determines that the participants must be sold, there are several approaches to consider:

- Put it in writing.
- Talk to each person on an individual basis.
- Call a meeting.

There are advantages and disadvantages to each approach. In general, the written approach is not as good as the oral approach. The oral approach offers more possibilities for persuasion by the leader. It also offers the flexibility of adjusting to the reaction of the sellee. Additionally, it offers more opportunity for repetition, emphasis, overcoming objections, and tailoring the sales approach to the individual. However, the written approach is usually cheaper and faster.

Do—
Discuss only positive information that is geared to ignite enthusiasm at general meeting sessions.

In comparing a meeting to the individual contact approach, the main difference is the interaction among the participants. If the leader feels that interaction will help sell the idea, policy, or decision, the meeting is a good choice. If the interaction might make it more difficult to sell, the individual approach is best. The cost and speed for using the two approaches are typically about even.

Instructional Meeting

There are many approaches that can be used to train and develop people:

- reading books or articles
- attending correspondence courses
- coaching by the boss or other qualified person
- instructing individuals with or without a computer
- sending individuals to an outside training course
- conducting in-house training meetings.

All of the training approaches, if effective, can improve the knowledge, skill, attitude, and behavior of the trainee. Each has certain advantages and disadvantages related to the cost-benefit ratio.

Below are some of the benefits to consider when deciding whether to conduct in-house training meetings:

- A number of people (a minimum of 10) have common training needs.
- A training meeting can satisfy the needs.

- Qualified instructors are available from inside or outside the organization.
- Good facilities are available for the meetings.
- Time for the participants will be made available by their line managers, or the participants are willing to take the training on their own time, or the organization is willing to pay participants for attending on their own time.
- A qualified in-house person is willing and able to spend time to plan and coordinate the meetings.
- The benefits are worth the cost.

Problem-Solving Meeting

A problem-solving meeting has one objective: to solve a problem. If the leader happens to be the boss, the problem could be solved by the leader without calling a meeting. However, the leader might feel that a problem-solving meeting is desirable to get a better quality solution or better acceptance from the participants. For example, there may be a production problem that must be solved. The enthusiastic acceptance of the solution by subordinates might be an important factor in whether the solution works. Many bosses have made good decisions in solving problems only to discover that subordinates sabotage these decisions intentionally or otherwise because of their lack of acceptance of the solution. In cases of this type, problem solving might be a desirable reason for a meeting if the participants can help to solve the problem or carry it out. In his book *The Change Resistors*, George Odiorne (1981) wrote: "If you want people to accept a decision, give them a feeling of ownership." The problem-solving approach illustrates this concept of getting participation to increase acceptance.

Do—
Get problem solving done early in the meeting—via workshops or buzz sessions.

Information-Getting Meeting

If the leader wants to get information from others, a meeting seems to be the obvious method. The leader can call the people together and ask each person for ideas, reactions, accomplishments, problems, solutions, or other kinds of information. Other ways to get this information should also be considered. For example, the leader can ask each person to write down the information and send it back to the leader. If this will provide the necessary information, the individual reports would be much cheaper than a group meeting. If it is important for the others to know the ideas of each, the leader can provide copies of the written materials to each person concerned instead of holding a meeting. But if it is important to have interaction among the individuals concerned, then a meeting becomes the most desirable method. In addition, if the leader determines that more and better information can be obtained in a meeting, then a meeting would be the most desirable method.

One specific example of a meeting to get information is called *brainstorming*. The slogan for a brainstorming meeting is *Think up or Shut up*. The purpose is to generate a large quantity of ideas. Freewheeling is encouraged, and judgment is forbidden. Ideas could also be solicited on an individual basis without having a meeting. But the meeting provides an opportunity for hitchhiking—one person's ideas stimulate ideas from others. If this interaction among the participants is important, then a meeting is the best method.

Comparing the Benefits and the Costs

During World War II, Ernie Pyle, a famous war correspondent, was asked by the military to help solve the problem of Nazi submarines in the Atlantic. Military spokespeople told Ernie of the problems the Nazis were causing by torpedoing American troop and merchant ships. After thinking a few moments, Ernie said, "Boil the ocean. Submarines can't operate in boiling water."

A military spokesperson replied, "But Ernie, how can we ever do that?"

Ernie replied, "I've given you the solution. You work out the details!"

It's easy to say that benefits should be compared to costs, but it's something else to actually compare the two. However, the cost-benefit comparison should be attempted as objectively as possible.

If, after careful consideration, a decision is made that in-house training meetings are undesirable but training needs exist, then alternative training approaches should be used.

When Is a Meeting Productive?

After a meeting adjourns, comments from participants may vary from "That was an excellent meeting" to "That meeting was a waste of time." Frequently, the leader feels that it was a productive meeting because the objectives were accomplished, but participants who attended feel that the meeting was nonproductive and ineffective. Why? Because there is a difference of opinion on what constitutes a productive meeting.

The first criterion for a productive meeting: *Were the objectives accomplished?* This assumes, of course, that the objectives of the meeting were worthwhile. These are usually determined by the leader.

The second criterion for a productive meeting: *Were the objectives accomplished in minimum time?* This criterion is more difficult to determine. Some participants think that comments, reactions, and discussion are necessary. Other participants may feel that this is a complete waste of time. And the leader may not be sure which is right.

The third criterion for a productive meeting: *Are the participants satisfied?* This doesn't mean that they have to be happy about the subject of the meeting or about the decisions that were reached. For example, the objective may be to communicate to the participants that there are going to be layoffs. Those in the meeting may have to reduce their staffs. Obviously, the participants will not be happy. They may be satisfied, however, if they understand the reasons for the layoffs and have a chance to raise questions and perhaps suggest alternative solutions to the problem of excessive costs. To get satisfied participants, it may be necessary to allow time for free and open discussion.

There are three necessary criteria for a meeting to be productive:

1. The objectives were accomplished.
2. The meeting was conducted in minimum time.
3. The participants were satisfied.

It becomes obvious that *minimum time* and *satisfied participants* present a dilemma for the leader. Whenever the leader concludes a meeting and says, "I accomplished my objectives in minimum time," the other question must also be asked: "Are the participants satisfied with the meeting?"

Chapter 12 describes how these three criteria can be evaluated.

Chapter 2

The Costs and Causes of a Nonproductive Meeting

═══ ➤

Expert and consultant on time management, R. Alec Mackenzie, conducted a study to determine the most significant timewasters in industry, business, and government. Table 2-1 lists timewaster profiles of five specific groups he studied. Each participant was asked to make a list of the top 10 personal timewasters in order of importance. The "No." column indicates the total number of participants who listed that item in their top 10 list. The "Wt." column shows the total weights (10 = most important) given by those who selected that item.

In summarizing his research on timewasters, Mackenzie ranked the top 10 in order of significance:

1. Telephone interruptions
2. Drop-in visitors
3. Meetings
4. Crises
5. Lack of objectives, priorities, and deadlines
6. Cluttered desk and personal disorganization
7. Ineffective delegation and involvement in routine and detail
8. Attempting too much at once and unrealistic time estimates
9. Lack of clear communication or instruction
10. Inadequate, inaccurate, and delayed information

Table 2-1. Timewaster Profile.

125 Major Food Corporation Managers	No.	Wt.
1. Crises/shifting priorities	66	196
2. Meetings	43	125
3. Lack of objectives, priorities, and deadlines	55	113
4. Telephone interruptions	38	108
5. Ineffective delegation and involvement in routine and detail	36	94
6. Drop-in visitors	43	90
7. Confused responsibility and authority	38	88
8. Inability to say "no"	31	75
9. Indecision/procrastination	24	63
10. Untrained, inadequate staff	13	45
11. Lack of clear communication or instruction	15	44
12. Socialization	14	40
13. Cluttered desk and personal disorganization	16	35
14. Inadequate, inaccurate, and delayed information	9	28
15. Attempting too much at once and unrealistic time estimates	11	26
16. Wanting all the facts	11	25
17. Lack of progress reviews	6	14
18. Multiple bosses	4	13
19. Failure to deal with poor performance	6	12
20. Overcontrol	2	10
21. Personnel changes	3	10

60 Electronic Communications Corporation Managers	No.	Wt.
1. Lack of objectives, priorities, and deadlines	38	118
2. Crises/shifting priorities	26	87
3. Drop-in visitors	30	75
4. Attempting too much at once and unrealistic time estimates	27	72
5. Indecision/procrastination	25	66
6. Lack of clear communication or instruction	22	65
7. Telephone interruptions	23	63
8. Ineffective delegation and involvement in routine and detail	24	59
9. Cluttered desk and personal disorganization	15	54
10. Confused responsibility and authority	17	45
11. Meetings	15	36
12. Socialization	10	26
13. Inadequate/untrained staff	10	25

75 School Administrators	No.	Wt.
1. Ineffective delegation and involvement in routine and detail	31	69
2. Telephone interruptions	30	57
3. Meetings	22	49
4. Drop-in visitors	19	42
5. Crises/firefighting/shifting priorities	18	33
6. Lack of objectives, priorities, and deadlines	13	30
7. Confused responsibilities	10	17
8. Paperwork	4	9
9. Indecision/procrastination	5	8
10. Lack of clear communication or instruction	3	8

50 Hospital Administrators	No.	Wt.
1. Telephone interruptions	40	164
2. Drop-in visitors	27	104
3. Ineffective delegation and involvement in routine and detail	34	89
4. Meetings	23	72
5. Inadequate/understaffed secretarial help	16	49
6. Lack of objectives, priorities, and deadlines	18	44
7. Attempting too much at once and unrealistic time estimates	19	43
8. Socialization	9	32
9. Cluttered desk and personal disorganization	12	31
10. Crises/switching priorities	13	29
11. Unable to say "no"	11	28
12. Inadequate, inaccurate, and delayed information	8	27
13. Procrastination/indecision	11	23
14. Lack of job description/duplication of effort/confused responsibilities/ responsibility without authority	8	23
15. Lack of teamwork/team conflict	7	20
16. Lack of clear communication or instruction	7	18
17. Lack of standards and conflicts/lack of feedback/failure to manage by exception	9	17
18. Failure to deal with poor performance	5	15
19. Lack of procedures and policies	4	11
20. Personnel problems	2	10

(continued on page 10)

Table 2-1. Timewaster Profile (continued).

26 Women Managers	No.	Wt.
1. Telephone interruptions	25	60
2. Drop-in visitors	14	51
3. Crises/attempting too much/switching priorities	16	40
4. Responsibility without authority/confused responsibility/two bosses/lack of job description/duplication of effort	8	35
5. Ineffective delegation and involvement in routine and detail	10	33
6. Understaffed/no secretary	4	14
7. Incomplete information/lack of communication/lack of feedback	5	13
8. Meetings	2	7
9. Lack of objectives, priorities, and deadlines	2	7
10. Stacked desk/team conflict/unable to say "no"/socialization	1	4

Don't—
discuss, in general sessions, subjects that are of interest to only a portion of the group. Allow time for special interest sessions.

According to supervisors and managers, the average amount of wasted time is between 10 percent and 50 percent, depending on the type of meeting. The highest percentage comes from those who attend departmental and staff meetings. The lowest percentage is for training meetings.

Very seldom do people try to determine the cost of a meeting. For anyone interested, a machine, the Econometer, has been built to help compute the cost. It's a Danish-built machine designed to cut down on management meeting addiction by computing the total cost of meetings minute by minute. It considers the number of participants and their average annual salary. Installed in a conference room, the Econometer operates like an electricity meter— the higher the power consumption, the faster the disk rotates and the higher the bill becomes. The hourly prices of the meetings are set on two digital switches: the adjustment range is from $10 to $990 per hour, and the scoreboard covers meeting costs up to $9,900. The same kind of figures could be computed without a machine. And these kinds of figures would make a leader think twice before calling a meeting.

It's much more difficult (if not impossible) to compute the benefits that are derived from a meeting. Usually, the best that can be done is to evaluate subjectively the possible benefits in terms of better results that come from a productive meeting.

To realize the importance of making meetings as productive as possible, look at the waste of time and money if meetings are not effective. Chapter 1 lists three ingredients that make a meeting productive: Objectives are accomplished in minimum time with satisfied participants. Consider the cost if any one of these ingredients is not achieved.

Objectives Were Not Accomplished

The meeting was a failure. To calculate the cost of the meeting, multiply the salary of each person by the time spent and arrive at a dollar cost of the meeting. In addition, add the cost of the time of the leader plus the direct costs of the facilities, materials, aids, food, and so forth.

There may have been some side benefits that would have to be considered, but overall the meeting was a failure and all (or nearly all) of the costs are lost.

Time Was Wasted

Guesstimate the amount of wasted time, and multiply it by the salaries of the attendees to arrive at a dollar figure. Add the cost of other activities that could have been done if the time was not wasted and the meeting ended sooner. Also, add some indirect costs that come from participants who are annoyed and frustrated when time is wasted. It isn't always easy to judge wasted time because there is often a difference of opinion concerning it. For example, if a participant gives a lengthy comment that was not pertinent or could have been said in a few words, the leader or another participant could say it was a waste of time. The participant, however, might have felt that the lengthy explanation was necessary.

Perhaps the best way to determine wasted time is to ask, *Did it help to contribute to the accomplishment of the objective?* If not, the time was probably wasted.

Participants Were Not Satisfied

The third ingredient of an effective meeting presents a new dimension in judging wasted time.

What is the cost of dissatisfaction on the part of people who leave a meeting? There is no way of measuring it in dollars and cents. However, the cost might be much greater than those costs previously mentioned. Some or all of the following factors may be present:

- A participant might resolve
  — I won't come to the next meeting.
  — I won't participate in future meetings if I'm forced to be there.

- A participant might determine
  — The leader is ineffective as a person (unprepared, unqualified, inefficient, arbitrary, etc.). This can affect future relationships with the leader and even the department that the leader represents.
  — Meetings are a waste of time, and we ought to eliminate them.

All of these thoughts point to negative attitudes and low morale on the part of the participants. These attitudes can result in costly behavior, such as poor productivity, complaints to other people, negative attitudes in future meetings, and even turnover.

Chapter 3

How to Coordinate a Meeting

Many meetings have a coordinator or chairperson who has responsibilities different from those of a leader. (For a discussion of the leader's role, see chapter 5.) For example, the role of the coordinator may be to plan the meeting and introduce a speaker or conference leader.

Following are some of the details needed to carry out the duties and responsibilities.

Before the Meeting

Good planning and preparation are necessary to have a productive meeting. Chapter 4 provides some of the detailed preparations that must be made. In addition, some special planning is necessary to select and orient the speaker or conference leader. Because the speaker is the single most important ingredient of a productive meeting, great care must be taken to select the right person and properly orient that person to the group and the objectives.

Specific duties and responsibilities of a meeting coordinator may include the following:

Before the Meeting
- deciding on the time and place
- selecting the participants
- determining the objectives
- selecting the speaker
- orienting the speaker
- notifying the participants

During the Meeting
- starting the meeting
- introducing the speaker
- controlling the meeting
- concluding the meeting

After the Meeting
- evaluating the meeting
- communicating with the speaker
- sending the minutes to participants
- conducting other necessary follow-up.

Selecting the Speaker

Determine what qualifications are most important. Typical ones are

- knowledge of the subject
- ability to communicate effectively with the participants
- availability
- fee and expenses within budgetary limitations.

It is easy to determine the availability and fee and expense requirements by simply asking the person. Before doing this, however, the coordinator should be sure that the other qualifications are met by the speaker. Knowledge of the subject is usually readily available because of the reputation of the individual. Also, the coordinator can ask the potential speaker if he or she is knowledgeable in the subject. The answer is usually reliable.

The most difficult and most critical factor to determine is the speaker's ability to communicate effectively with the participants. Many coordinators have used unreliable methods such as seeing the name on someone else's programs or, even worse, knowing that the person has written a book or article. A better method is to talk or write to the potential speaker and get details on previous meetings, including subject and nature of group. Then check with someone who has personally heard the speaker to get first-hand reactions. Ask specific questions related to the subject, participants, objectives, and reactions. Describe your situation and ask how well the speaker would perform under your circumstances.

These approaches are only substitutes for the best way to select a speaker, which is to hear the person speak. This should be done whenever practical. And the more you have at stake (for example, top executives, a lengthy program, critical participants), the more important it becomes to screen the speaker by first-hand reaction.

Orienting the Speaker

Almost equal in importance to the selection is the orientation of the speaker to your own situation. A personal visit is the best way to accomplish this. Next best is a telephone call. If neither of these is practical, written communication can also do the job. The items covered in orienting a speaker should

- Clarify the objectives of the overall meeting or program and the specific objectives to be accomplished by the speaker.
- Clarify what comes before and after the speaker.

- Describe the participants, including their positions in the organization, their levels of knowledge and experience related to the subject being presented, their attitudes toward the subject, and any special circumstances or problems they have that are related to the subject.
- Define the place of the meeting.
- Determine the exact amount of time that the speaker is responsible for—starting and quitting time.
- Suggest an approach for the speaker to take. For example, you might suggest a 30-minute talk to be followed by 15 minutes of questions. Or you might suggest the presentation of a case study or a film to be followed by group discussion. Your suggested approach should be discussed with the speaker to see if the speaker agrees or has an approach that will work better. (When I've been asked to talk to a professional group, I'm typically told to speak for 45 minutes and allow 15 minutes for questions and answers. I suggest—and usually follow—an entirely different format and still stay within the 60-minute time period. My approach includes discussion or involvement throughout the talk.)

> **Do—**
> Make every presentation to the point; don't ramble.

- Offer to help with handout materials, audiovisual aids, special room setup, hotel reservations, or any other special requests from the speaker.

I recently had a rare opportunity to be oriented effectively by the coordinator of a program. I was asked by Howard Frankel, coordinator of employee development for Panhandle Eastern Pipeline Company, to conduct a workshop for 140 supervisors and managers on the effective implementation of change. The afternoon prior to my workshop, some dramatic changes were going to be announced by top management. The changes concerned reorganization, diversification, possible acquisitions, new projects, and possible joint ventures with a foreign country. The most dramatic change was in the reorganization, which became more centralized. A number of people's jobs and locations would be affected. Howard and the top management people decided that proper orientation was to have me attend the meeting in which the changes were announced and listen to the question-and-answer period that followed dinner that evening. As a result, I became thoroughly familiar with the attendees' issues, jargon, and feelings. It helped me relate more effectively with those who were most affected by the changes. This first-hand orientation was invaluable to my conducting an effective session on the following day.

During the Meeting

There are two important functions to be performed by the coordinator that have not been discussed in other parts of this manual:

1. introducing a speaker or conference leader
2. controlling a meeting when someone else (speaker or conference leader) is leading the meeting.

Do—
Use natural enthusiasm, not artificial props.

Introducing a Speaker

Despite all that's been spoken and written on how to introduce a speaker, most introductions are mediocre at best. They do not accomplish what an introduction should do, namely, convince the audience that this is the right person to serve as speaker or conference leader. And a poor introduction can create a negative attitude on the part of the speaker or the audience.

CHARACTERISTICS OF AN EFFECTIVE INTRODUCTION

Every introduction should include two factors:

1. The introducer is enthused. The audience will readily pick up the enthusiasm—or lack of it—exhibited by the introducer.
2. The introducer explains why this speaker on this subject. If the speaker has been properly selected, this part is easy. The introducer should be able to tell the following facts concerning the speaker:

   - knowledge of subject
     Illustrations: education, experience, books read, and publications
   - ability to communicate effectively
     Illustrations: previous talks, future talks scheduled, and personal testimonies of the introducer if the introducer has heard the speaker
   - knowledge of audience
     Illustrations: speaker's experience that is similar to that of the audience, talks to similar groups, knows members of audience personally, or introducer has told speaker about the audience
   - other information that would be of interest to the audience
     Illustrations: recent travel (Europe, Japan, etc.), hobbies (bowled a 300 game), family situation (10 children), or special honors (president of a professional society).

THE RIGHT LENGTH FOR AN INTRODUCTION

I've often been introduced by a person who says, "I don't want to take any of the speaker's time by giving a long introduction, so I'll just turn the meeting right over to Don Kirkpatrick."

This is usually another way of saying, "I haven't prepared an introduction, so I'll get off the hook by cleverly turning the meeting over immediately."

In terms of the length of the introduction, it shouldn't be too long; likewise, it shouldn't be too short. It's difficult to indicate the minimum or maximum number of minutes. Rather, it should be judged by two criteria:

1. Does it tell the audience why you have selected this speaker on this subject?
2. Does it maintain the audience's attention while doing it?

This of course adds the dimension of manner of introduction with the content. Some introducers can create boredom and impatience on the part of the audience in a 15-second introduction; other introducers can maintain a high degree of interest for five minutes by using the right information and entering a note of humor and enthusiasm.

THE MANNER OF INTRODUCTION

Enthusiasm is the key to the manner in which an introduction should be made. Another characteristic is good eye contact with the audience. There is no excuse for reading an introduction. Some notes are all right, but the introducer should be properly prepared so that eye contact can be maintained. If the speaker has written a book, the introducer should have the book in hand to show it to the audience. The final words of the introduction should be the subject of the talk and the name of the speaker. When this is done, the introducer should turn the meeting over to the speaker and leave the stage. Preferably, the introducer should head to the back of the meeting room where he or she can properly observe and, if necessary, help control the meeting.

Controlling the Meeting

Chapter 9 discusses the methods and techniques for controlling a meeting. The approach was based on the presumption that the person in charge of the meeting was the speaker or conference leader.

The role of the coordinator becomes quite different and probably more difficult when a speaker is leading the meeting. For example, the speaker may be very pleased with the meeting and feels it is completely under control. But the coordinator, sitting in the back of the room, may think that it is completely out of control. When this type of problem arises, what becomes the role of the coordinator?

Controlling a meeting when the coordinator is not the speaker is a tough situation that must be handled carefully—but yet handled. Here are some typical situations and suggested actions to take:

The Situation	Action To Be Taken by Coordinator
Leader gets off the subject	Interrupt the speaker tactfully, and draw attention to the subject being discussed.
Group is becoming bored or restless	Interrupt the meeting by taking a break, inserting thoughts or ideas, suggesting a buzz group, or initiating a change of pace.
One participant is dominating to the detriment of the meeting	Interrupt and handle the situation.
Leader is running past allotted time	Give a warning (two minutes, etc.), or cut it off by indicating, "Time is up, and the leader will stay around to answer questions."

These situations indicate some difficult control problems that have been encountered by coordinators. Usually, there is a reluctance to interrupt or otherwise assume control for fear of embarrassing and even alienating the speaker and perhaps some participants. However, to have a productive meeting, the coordinator must take action, even at the risk of making the speaker unhappy.

Concluding the Meeting

Chapter 9 details principles and approaches for concluding a meeting. Here are some additional points to stress when the coordinator is not the leader.

The coordinator should be constantly aware of the importance of concluding the meeting on time. The problem of the speaker's running overtime is a very common one and must be delicately handled by the coordinator. If this situation was foreseen, the coordinator should have made some prearranged agreement with the speaker to provide a warning. A large card that says "5 MINUTES" could be held up in the back of the room to alert the speaker. Perhaps a "2 MINUTES" card is also needed or possibly one that says "10 MINUTES."

Do—
Start on time; stay on time; end on time.

The coordinator should always conclude the meeting instead of having the speaker do it. In the conclusion, the coordinator should thank the speaker. This thanks should be as specific as possible in terms of the contribution that was made. It should also be honest.

Here are some examples of coordinator conclusions:

- **An Instructional Meeting** *(an excellent meeting)*
  "On behalf of the Management Institute, University of Wisconsin, I'd like to thank you, Bill, for the excellent job you did. We appreciate your enthusiasm and the practical approach you used. We also appreciate the excellent handouts you provided for the group. We hope you can come back for a repeat performance soon."

- **A Speech** *(dry but informative)*
  "Thanks, Ben, for conducting the meeting for us. You've provided a lot of information for us to think about. We appreciate your time and effort to make this a beneficial program."

- **A Speech** *(stimulating and interesting)*
  "Thanks, Tom, for your excellent talk. We appreciate the special efforts you made to be here and talk to this group. Also, your approach has provided a challenge for each of us as we go back to our jobs. I think that each of us has not only some practical ideas but also a good story or two that we can use. Thanks again for a most stimulating and informative talk. I hope we can have you back again soon."

- **A Speech** *(informative but poorly presented)*
  "Thanks, Harry, for the very informative talk. I know that you spent a lot of time preparing for the meeting. And we appreciate all of the data that you presented."

In concluding the meeting the coordinator should also

- Restate the objective of the meeting
- Summarize the accomplishments
- Thank participants for coming
- Thank the group for their participation/contribution
- Give assignments
- Announce the next meeting
- Have the group complete evaluation sheets.

After the Meeting

Chapter 12 provides detailed suggestions on how to evaluate a meeting. The coordinator or chairperson may well be the trained observer who evaluates the meeting. This evaluation should be communicated to the leader as candidly and specifically as possible. If there are critical comments, tact is essential to avoid resentment on the part of the leader or speaker. To supplement this trained observer's evaluation, reactions should also be obtained from participants. These reactions and comments should also be communicated to the leader.

In addition to evaluating the speaker, participants may need to be refreshed on the purpose of the meeting. Sending minutes of the meeting or a summary is generally a good idea. It helps to clarify and remind participants of what was accomplished. It can also communicate to those who did not attend the meeting.

Chapter 4

How to Prepare for a Meeting

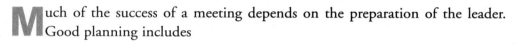

Much of the success of a meeting depends on the preparation of the leader. Good planning includes

- determining the objectives to be accomplished
- selecting the participants
- knowing the participants
- choosing the time
- selecting the place
- creating the agenda
- determining the physical arrangements
- sending notice to participants
- making the final preparations.

Determining the Objectives To Be Accomplished

In deciding on whether a meeting should be held, objectives must be considered. However, the objectives are usually not clarified at the time when the decision has been made to hold a meeting. Therefore, the leader must determine the exact objectives to be accomplished. If, for example, an information-giving meeting is planned, the objectives to be accomplished might be one or more of the following:

- Participants will understand the new vacation policy.
- Participants will understand the status of a project.
- Participants will understand a change in methods, including
  — reasons for the change
  — the new method.

You will notice that all of these objectives are oriented to the participants instead of to the leader. These objectives are clearer and better than if the objectives had been stated

- to describe the new vacation policy
- to give a status report on the project
- to discuss a methods change.

If the purpose of the meeting is to solve a problem, the objectives could be stated as:

- How can scrap be reduced from 5 percent to 3 percent by December 1?
- How can overtime be reduced to 3 percent of total direct costs by July 1?
- How can turnover be reduced by 30 percent by September 1?
- How can sales be increased by 5 percent by December 31?
- How can customer complaints be reduced by 10 percent by July 1?
- How can profits be increased by 3 percent by December 31?

All of these objectives are stated in specific terms so that the problem is clear. The meeting would not be productive until the specific objectives had been met. In these examples, decisions must be reached in the meeting on specifically what to do to accomplish the objectives.

If the purpose of the meeting is to brainstorm a subject, possible objectives could be

- What are all the possible ways to reduce tardiness?
- What are all the possible ways to reduce costs?
- What are all the possible ways to recruit new technical employees?
- What are all the possible ways to get new customers?
- What are all the possible ways to improve service to customers?

Objectives must be determined in advance and must be clear to the leader. These objectives should be stated in terms of what should be accomplished, not what should be done. And they should always be as specific as possible.

Selecting the Participants

When the objectives have been determined, the leader must select the participants to attend the meeting. There are two basic criteria for deciding who should be at the meeting:

1. those who can benefit enough to be worth their time
2. those who can contribute enough to justify their time.

Both of these criteria require subjective judgment on the part of the leader. Sometimes the leader would determine that a particular person could benefit by getting information. But the leader might also determine that the information could be given to the person after the meeting and, thereby, save the time of the person. Likewise, the leader could determine that a person could contribute an idea or two by attending. But the leader might also realize that the idea could be obtained from the person before the meeting and eliminate the need for that person being at the meeting.

There is a third criterion that should also be considered by the leader: those who want to be at the meeting.

Some people want to be there to satisfy their egos. Others want to be there to get firsthand knowledge of what happens in the meeting. In some cases, a strong negative attitude may develop if a particular individual is not invited to the meeting. The leader must decide whether to invite individuals to the meeting just because they want to be there.

Knowing the Participants

The leader should have knowledge of the participants. As a minimum, the leader should know what departments and jobs they represent. The leader should also know their levels of knowledge of subjects to be discussed. Also, the leader would benefit from knowing their interest in the subject as well as their need to know.

If the objective of the meeting is instruction, more knowledge of participants is required by the leader. The instructor should know such things as attitudes, problems, and previous training that the participants have had.

Don't—
Bore the participants.

Before each meeting, leaders should ask themselves, "What should I know about the participants to accomplish the meeting objectives?" Preparation by the leaders should include the acquiring of this knowledge.

Choosing the Time

The selection of the meeting time is very important. The first consideration should be given to the availability of the leader and enough time for adequate preparation. Just as important is the availability of the participants and their preference for a particular time. If participants have a negative attitude toward the time, the leader will have a

Don't—
Get too elementary.
Keep it practical.

more difficult time accomplishing the objectives. Participants with negative attitudes are not very eager to understand information that is presented or to participate in problem solving.

The best way to select the right time is to ask meeting participants for their preference. Employees of one company encouraged their boss to conduct regular staff meetings every two weeks. The boss agreed to do it and asked them, "When is the best time?" The boss surveyed the group for both availability and preference and selected Tuesday at 9 a.m. as the best time.

The selection of meeting time should include both the starting and concluding times. If the length of the meeting can be predicted and controlled (i.e., an instructional meeting), the quitting time should be determined and announced to the participants. If the length of the meeting is unpredictable (i.e., a problem-solving meeting), the approximate length of the meeting should be determined and communicated to the participants.

I was asked to conduct a series of five training meetings for the foremen and supervisors of a Racine, Wisconsin, corporation. We agreed on five sessions of three and one-half hours each. Each session would be conducted twice so that all three shifts could attend. They decided that the best schedule would be on Monday through Friday from 7 a.m. to 10:30 a.m. and from 3 p.m. to 6:30 p.m.

Racine is about 90 minutes from my home in Elm Grove. And what do you do in Racine from 10:30 a.m. to 3 p.m. for five straight days? If they had asked me for a suggested schedule, I would have said 8:30 a.m. to noon and 1 p.m. to 4:30 p.m. But they didn't ask me; they told me!

The reason they picked the schedule was because it was the best time for all three shift foremen and supervisors to attend. And I had to make the best of it. The schedule must fit the desire and convenience of those who will attend and their bosses, not necessarily the trainer.

Selecting the Place

Many leaders pick the most convenient place to hold a meeting. Frequently, this is a bad choice. Several factors should be considered in selecting the right place:

- availability of the room at the time of the meeting
- large enough to comfortably accommodate the participants as well as any audiovisual aids
- appropriate furniture, including tables and chairs (the longer the meeting, the greater the need for comfortable chairs)
- adequate lights and ventilation

- free from interruptions and distractions, including noise and telephones
- convenience for participants
- cost.

Sometimes several of these criteria are in conflict with each other. For example, it may be convenient for participants and also free of charge to hold a meeting on company premises. However, the facilities may be too small or too close to the offices of participants, which could lead to distractions (mental and physical) as well as interruptions.

Do—
Check the facilities for problems, such as lighting and sound capabilities.

The selection of a place is very important because the attitudes of participants are affected. Leaders have more difficulty accomplishing objectives if participants have such negative attitudes as, "It's too crowded," "It's too noisy," "It's too hot," or "The chairs are too hard."

Incidentally, an ad appeared in *Forbes* magazine, stating, "Over 90 percent of our clients report that using our conference center increases the productivity of their meetings." I don't know how accurate the statement is, but it does emphasize the importance of good facilities.

Creating the Agenda

Some leaders confuse agenda with objectives. Objectives are subjects to be accomplished. The agenda is the order in which the subjects will be covered.

Many meetings have several objectives. For example, a staff or departmental meeting may include an item of information to be communicated to participants. It may also include information getting in which the leader wants to find out the status of a project. It may even include a problem-solving objective.

In preparing for the meeting, the leader must consider the objectives and prepare the agenda. For a typical staff meeting, the following might be included on the agenda:

- introduction of Jim Tohomos, a new staff member
- update on safety record
- status report on Project 571
- new reporting procedure on absences and tardiness
- update on quality and scrap
- the next meeting time and location.

In planning the meeting, the leader should determine who should be there for each item on the agenda. If one or more of the participants don't have to be there for part of the meeting, the agenda should be established so those participants don't have to attend all of the meeting. Perhaps they can leave after the fourth item has been discussed.

In some cases, a particular person is needed for only one item on the agenda. Either this can be the first item or else the person can be on a standby basis and can be called when needed.

These kinds of preparations are very useful in reducing or even eliminating time wasted by people who are not interested or involved in certain parts of a meeting.

Determining the Physical Arrangements

In preparing physical arrangements, the leader must consider objectives as well as the number of participants who will attend. If it is an information-giving meeting with many participants, then theater style (without tables) may be the best physical arrangement. However, if there are five participants in a problem-solving meeting, the best room setup is to have people sit around a table so they can all see and hear each other.

Do—
Have the meeting room properly set up, not only to show the theme, but also to indicate the meeting is well conceived and not just thrown together at the last moment.

If the meeting is for training and instruction purposes, several effective approaches are possible. In fact, the physical arrangement may be varied for different meetings in a training program to best accomplish the specific objectives of that meeting.

As an example, two departments at the University of Wisconsin use seminar room setups that are quite different, as shown in figure 4-1.

Careful preparation of physical arrangements should include

- table and chairs and the proper setup to accomplish the meeting objectives
- decisions on smoking, such as
  — Is smoking allowed? If yes, ashtrays must be provided.
    (Note: In nearly all meetings, smoking is not allowed.)
  — Should nonsmokers be considered? If yes, a special section or nonsmokers' tables should be designated.
- water for participants, if the length of the meeting warrants it
- table name cards, if appropriate, so that the leader can use names of participants and participants can get acquainted with each other
- audiovisual equipment as needed (A flipchart, whiteboard, or overhead projector should be standard equipment to clarify information from the

Figure 4-1. The University of Wisconsin Room Set-Ups.

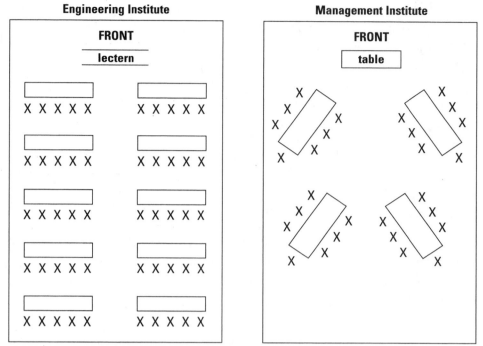

leader and to record ideas from participants. Be sure that all aids are ready and in good working order.)

● scheduled breaks, if the length of the meeting warrants them. (If meetings last more than an hour and a half, a break should be scheduled. Coffee or soft drinks should be provided. These breaks can have a valuable effect on the attitudes of participants and the effectiveness of the meeting.)

Sending Notice to Participants

Few meeting leaders give appropriate notice to the participants. Sometimes it's because there isn't enough time between the decision to have the meeting and the time of the meeting. The most frequent reason for no or inadequate notice is because the leader neglects to do it.

Proper notice is necessary so participants can plan to be there and do whatever preparation is necessary. Also, proper advance notice creates positive attitudes on the part of the participants by making them feel important and also impressed with the planning of the meeting leader.

Do—
Issue in advance a program schedule and topics.

Here are the five main items that should be included in an advance notice to participants:

1. time (starting and quitting, unless it is a problem-solving meeting in which a quitting time is only suggested)
2. place
3. objectives
4. preparation to be done by participants
5. names of other participants.

The notice should be sent far enough in advance so that participants can reserve the time and make preparations.

Making the Final Preparations

There are always some final arrangements that can make the difference between a productive and a nonproductive meeting. Leaders sometimes do an effective job of planning and, yet, something goes wrong. To avoid this, final attention should be given to

- the physical facilities (Check to be sure everything is set. The leader should be at the meeting room 30 to 60 minutes before the start of the meeting to take care of any last-minute problems.)
- the audiovisual equipment (Check to be sure it works properly.)
- the materials (The leader should be sure that all materials are ready, including handouts, name cards, paper, and notebooks.)
- attendance of participants. (If necessary, phone calls or emails should be sent to participants to remind them of the time and place. This is especially important if the original notice was sent out a considerable time in advance of the meeting.)

For details on the many preparations that can possibly go wrong, see Appendix E. An analysis of these preparations will help leaders in their own preparations to be sure that these catastrophes do not occur.

Chapter 5

The Role of the Leader

Item 14 of the pretest states, "A meeting leader is more effective as a catalyst than a strong leader."

Your answer will depend on your interpretation of "catalyst" and "strong leader." To answer the question, take a look at the role of the leader in different types of meetings, as shown in figure 5-1.

Information-Giving Meeting

In this type of meeting, the role of the leader is to communicate the information so that the group understands. Figure 5-1 shows that a meeting might be 100 percent participation by the leader and 0 percent by the group. In other words, the leader does all the talking. Questions from the group might alter participation to 90 percent by the leader and 10 percent by the group.

Instructional Meeting

The role of the leader is one of teacher. The percentage of participation would depend on subject, objectives, and the knowledge and experience of the group, as well as on the personal style of the leader. For example, if the leader is an effective lecturer (speaker, presenter, etc.) and the group has little knowledge of the subject, the percentage may be 75-90 percent leader and 25-10 percent group.

If the leader prefers discussion, case studies, and management games, the figures may be evenly split, even if the group knows little about the subject.

If the group is knowledgeable in the subject, the leader may be 20 percent with 80 percent of the participation coming from the group.

Figure 5-1. Participation Chart.

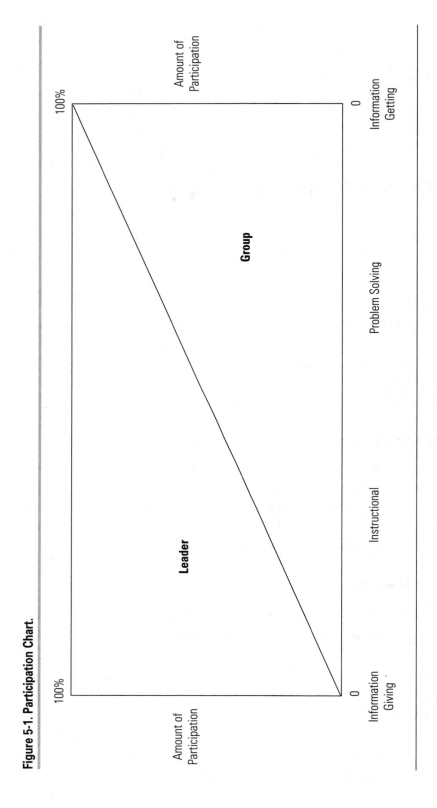

Problem-Solving Meeting

The leader's challenge is to guide the group in the best solution to the problem. In this kind of meeting, the leader would accomplish the following tasks:

- Present information (that is, a statement of the problem, why it is important to solve, and background information).
- Get all members of the group to participate in solving the problem.
- Present ideas that will be considered in solving the problem (the leader steps down from the leadership role and becomes an equal member of the group).
- Control the meeting so that it moves toward the accomplishment of the objective, with minimum loss of time, friction, conflict, and antagonism among the participants.
- Conclude the meeting with a summary of what was accomplished and what happens next.

> **Do—**
> Keep the meeting moving on a predetermined schedule.

The ratio for participation should be somewhere between 40-60 percent leader and 60-40 percent group.

Information-Getting Meeting

This kind of meeting requires an entirely different role by the leader. The leader must get attention and clarify objectives. In addition, the leader may provide some background information. The leader would probably participate 10-20 percent while the group dominates with 90-80 percent participation. The role of the leader is to get the group to participate and control the participation to accomplish the objective.

The role of the leader can vary dramatically. Sometimes, the role varies within the same meeting. For example, in a problem-solving meeting, the role includes presenter, stimulator, participant, and controller.

Now, look at the statement that began this section: "A meeting leader is more effective as a catalyst than a strong leader." *Webster's* defines *catalyst* as "substance that accelerates a reaction and is unchanged in the process." Based on this definition, the role of catalyst is appropriate in certain meetings and entirely inappropriate in others. It is appropriate for information-getting and brainstorming meetings

> **Do—**
> Involve participants as much as possible.

and in some sections of problem-solving and instructional meetings. It is inappropriate in informational meetings and some parts of problem-solving and instructional meetings.

If we ask various people to define *strong leader*, we will get many answers. Some people look at this as a negative term that means "domineering," "authoritarian," "arrogant," "bull of the woods," and "dictatorial." I consider it a positive term that connotes "control" and "flexibility." A strong leader is necessary to keep the meeting productive, which is to accomplish objectives in minimum time with satisfied participants. The leader must know when to lecture, dominate, and be the authority. The leader must also know when to serve in the role of catalyst, stimulator, and listener. Table 5-1 summarizes the role of the leader in each type of meeting.

Table 5-1. The Role of a Leader.

Information-Giving Meeting	Instructional Meeting	Problem-Solving Meeting	Information-Getting Meeting
1. Present information so it will be understood. 2. Answer questions from group.	1. Teach participants. 2. Instruct so that participants learn.	1. Present information so it will be understood. 2. Get group to participate in problem solving. 3. Participate as a member of the group. 4. Control meeting.	1. Present objective. 2. Stimulate participants to give their ideas. 3. Listen.

Chapter 6

The Question—
Uses and Misuses

The question is one of the most important tools that a leader must be able to use. In information-getting and problem-solving meetings, the leader must ask the right questions in the right way. In information-giving meetings, the leader must effectively answer questions. The failure to ask or answer questions effectively can turn a productive meeting into a nonproductive one.

Asking Questions

Here are 10 guidelines to follow:

> **Do—**
> In most meetings provide time for a question-and-answer period.

1. Prepare your questions ahead of time. Be sure they are clear and can be answered by one or more of the participants.
2. Use overhead questions frequently. These are questions that are directed to the group and require volunteers to answer.
3. Call the person by name first, and then state the question, when using a direct question. This alerts the person to concentrate on the question. The direct question should be used sparingly. When it is used, be sure the person can answer the question so that there is no embarrassment. A direct question would be appropriate when you see that a person is about ready to say something but doesn't quite have the courage to volunteer.
4. Avoid leading questions. These are questions that clearly indicate the answer you want. An example would be, "Don't you think that films of horrible accidents will make the workers operate their machines more safely?"

5. Allow participants time to think after asking questions (especially overhead questions). To answer, participants usually go through the following process:
    a. Analyze the question to be sure they understand.
    b. Think of an answer.
    c. Think of the proper wording of the answer.
    d. Evaluate the answer in terms of how the leader and the group will react to the answer. (The person who answers will usually try to avoid an answer that might get a negative reaction from the leader or the group.)

> The thinking process after a question has been asked takes time, and the leader should not become impatient because there is an embarrassing silence of 5 to 15 seconds when nobody responds. Some leaders get panicky and repeat the question or answer it themselves. When this happens, the thought process of the participant is interrupted and switches from thinking to listening.
>
> This embarrassing silence problem can be solved by doing something productive during that period of 5 to 15 seconds. Use this time to write the question on the whiteboard or flipchart. This not only takes up the time, but also helps the participants understand the question. After finishing the writing, the leader can turn to the group and ask, "Who wants to answer the question?" A number of participants will probably be ready to answer if the question has been carefully prepared.

6. Encourage complete and clearly expressed answers.
7. Be sincerely interested in the answers. If appropriate, write some key words from the answers on the whiteboard or flipchart. This demonstrates that you are listening and also interested. It also encourages answers from other participants.
8. Be sure that the same few people don't answer all the questions. One technique is to have all participants write down their answers. Then you can better control who answers the questions by directing the question to a specific person or by going around the room and asking each person for an answer.
9. Avoid questions that can be answered by "yes" or "no." If you use these, then follow up the answer with "Why do you feel that way?" or a similar question that encourages the reasons for the "yes" or "no."
10. Begin good questions that encourage meaningful answers with such words as
    • What: What solution do you suggest?
    • Why: Why do you feel that way?

- When: When did you first notice that Rose was unhappy with her job?
- Where: Where is the best place to conduct an appraisal interview?
- Who: Who is responsible to see that new employees are properly trained?
- How: How can we cut down on the cost of long distance telephone calls?

Answering Questions

Many leaders are so anxious to get questions from participants that they waste valuable time answering questions that should not be answered. Some questions are off the subject being discussed. Others are unique to the person asking the questions, and meeting time should not be used to answer them.

> **Don't—**
> Let one person dominate the whole show. Meetings seem to be a great place for self-styled leaders to preach endlessly.

These situations call attention to the fact that the leader should evaluate each question that is asked in terms of *Should I take time to answer the question?* This is often a difficult decision, and a frequent solution may be to answer it quickly to satisfy the person who asks it and yet not waste the time of the rest of the group. Another solution is to say that it is off the subject or not of general interest. This, of course, must be tactfully done. If the leader decides that the question should be answered, the next decision to make is *Who should answer it?*

Table 6-1 shows three alternatives to consider. Each of them may be appropriate for particular situations.

When a question is asked, the leader must quickly evaluate it to judge whether to spend time answering it. If it is off the subject, the leader can say, "That's a good question, but it doesn't fit in with our objective. I'll be glad to discuss it with you after the meeting." In any case, time should not be taken to answer questions that are not important to the meeting objectives.

If the leader decides to take time to answer it, the three alternatives in table 6-1 should be considered. Sometimes only one of them will be used. At other times, all three approaches may be used.

For questioning to be an effective instructional technique, create the proper atmosphere in which it can flourish. For example, trainees should never fear to give an incorrect answer. If wrong answers are discouraged, the trainees will respond more cautiously with generally poor answers to your questions. Trainees should never have the feeling that they're asking stupid questions. It cannot be overemphasized that they should be encouraged to ask questions, at any time, about anything they do not understand.

Table 6-1. Who Should Answer It?

Who Should Answer?	Under What Circumstances?
1. The leader	a. If the question has been asked directly of the leader. Even under these circumstances, the leader may decide not to answer it by saying, "Before I answer it, I'd like to see what others in the group feel." b. If the leader is the only one with the answer. c. If time is short and the leader wants to move along to another item.
2. Other members of the group	a. If other members of the group have answers. b. If other members of the group want to express their feelings. c. If time warrants it. d. If the leader doesn't want to answer or needs time to think of an answer. e. If the person asking the question wants the opinion of the group.
3. The person who asked the question	a. If the leader feels that the participant has something to say. (Oftentimes a question is asked in such a way that it is obvious that the person has strong feelings to express.) b. If the leader or the group doesn't know the answer. It should be turned back to the person who asked the question only if the leader feels that the person has an answer.

Chapter 7

How to Present Information Effectively

There are three keys to an effective presentation: preparation, presentation techniques, and audiovisual aids. The last of the three is not essential in all presentations, but in most meetings it is highly desirable. This section will consider these three factors that result in an effective presentation.

Before discussing the three keys, it is important to clarify what a leader must accomplish in a presentation. In the first place, the speaker must get the attention and interest of the audience. In other words, the speaker must create and maintain a desire for them to listen and understand. Next, the leader must communicate so they understand. In addition, the speaker may want to persuade and even get participants to take action.

Do—
Be well prepared. A good speaker should be able to cover every possible important point in minimum time.

Preparation

Good preparation by the speaker is essential. The amount of time required to prepare varies in relationship to such factors as speaker's experience, knowledge of subject, and knowledge of the audience. Some of the necessary preparations include

- Know the participants, including their interest in the subject, their level of knowledge of the subject, and their attitude toward it.
- Know the subject in enough depth to communicate it clearly and be able to answer pertinent questions about it.

- Know the specific objectives you want to accomplish, including
  — what you want them to understand
  — what attitude they should have toward the subject
  — what they are expected to do with the information.
- List all the topics you could present that could lead to the objective. Include general information, research, theory, examples, personal experiences, and ideas of others, such as authors and experts. In other words, list all of the topics you could discuss on the subject.
- Consider the amount of time you have to present the material and select those items that are most important to cover.
- Consider what audiovisual aids will help present the material. Remember that people usually understand better if they can see as well as hear.
- Prepare an outline as detailed as you need to present effectively. This would vary from a complete script for some people to a mental outline (nothing written) for others. (I wouldn't recommend either extreme unless you are a most experienced and unusual speaker.)

Your presentation should be divided into three sections:

1. introduction
2. body
3. conclusion.

The introduction should get the attention of the audience and clearly communicate the purpose of the talk. A dramatic example or story is one way of getting attention. Another is to convince the audience that they should listen.

The body of the presentation should present the material in proper sequence so the audience can understand it.

The conclusion should include a restatement of the objectives as well as a summary of what was presented. If appropriate, it should also include any assignments and clarification of "Now, what?"

An old preacher once described his approach to a sermon as, "Tell 'em what you are going to tell 'em, tell 'em, and tell 'em what you told 'em." It succinctly describes his introduction, body, and conclusion. Many speakers have adopted his philosophy for their presentations. It's good for getting an understanding and remembering through repetition. But it would be bad if the repetition loses the audience. Therefore, a variety in the way the material is presented is necessary if this philosophy is applied.

- Prepare all of your audiovisual aids, including charts, slides, overhead transparencies, Microsoft PowerPoint presentations, and handouts.
- Practice your talk if it is being given for the first or second time, perhaps into a tape recorder or in front of a live audience of one (your spouse?) or more. (Don't memorize it unless you are an unusual speaker with a perfect memory.)

Presentation Techniques

A good presentation requires two important qualities of the speaker: self-confidence and enthusiasm. Self-confidence usually comes with thorough preparation plus experience in giving talks. Therefore, leaders should look for opportunities to speak so that self-confidence can develop and improve. Enthusiasm comes from being convinced that the material will be of benefit to the audience. It is more than seriousness. It also includes a conviction that what is presented is true and right for the audience. In other words, the subject content must fit the audience's interests or needs. Enthusiasm may also include an inner quality that is difficult to develop.

Some other characteristics of effective presentations are

- eye contact with the audience (This usually means that the speaker reads as little as possible.)
- effective use of the pause to let a point sink in or to wait for audience reaction
- effective use of anecdotes or examples that are real to the audience (This is an important part of preparation. It is also important that the presentation be well made. For example, a story should be told and not read.)
- variety in the tone, inflection, pitch, and volume of the voice (Nothing turns an audience away like a monotone voice.)
- wise use of humor (Some people can tell stories effectively. They should do it. Others can't tell them well and should avoid them. Needless to say, the story should be appropriate for the audience without offending anyone. There is no excuse at any time for telling a dirty story or one that offends people.)
- avoidance of distracting mannerisms (This is a most difficult characteristic to define. Some speakers can walk around and throw up their hands wildly without distracting an audience. In fact, it helps them maintain interest and attention and increases understanding. Other speakers can walk a few

feet from the lectern and then walk back and the audience is distracted. The gestures of some speakers are natural, and the same gestures by other presenters seem unnatural and are distractions.)

Distracting Mannerisms

Some speakers use such words as "uh" very frequently but no one notices. Others can use half as many uhs, and it bothers the audience to the point that they start counting the uhs and don't hear another thing. Some leaders can jingle coins in their pockets and not be noticed while others will do it and completely lose the audience.

The best way to avoid distracting mannerisms is to learn which of your mannerisms distract the audience and then quit doing them. A trained observer in the back of the room can help you learn your distracting mannerisms. The other approach is to make your presentation so interesting that the audience is listening so hard that they don't notice the mannerisms. This is probably the reason why the mannerisms of one speaker are not distracting while the same ones by another speaker completely lose the audience.

- the right choice of words (Speak the language of the audience.)
- short sentences (Don't use long, involved sentences.)
- visuals used as notes (If you use such visuals as overhead transparencies, handouts, and Microsoft PowerPoint presentations, let these be your notes. Don't try to follow your written notes and use these kinds of visuals at the same time.)
- capitalization on strengths and avoidance of weaknesses. (This summarizes many of the previous characteristics and simply means "Be yourself." It's OK to observe effective speakers and see what makes them effective. It's also a good idea to use some of their approaches and methods. But don't try to copy their personalities. Develop a style of your own.)

Don't—
Give dull, monotonous talks that are read meticulously from scripts.

Audiovisual Aids

Some speakers are very effective in maintaining interest and creating understanding without the use of aids. A combination of enthusiasm, humor, examples, and unusual speaking ability is usually present.

Most presenters can be more effective by using aids to supplement their oral presentations. Visual aids add the sense of sight to that of hearing and usually assist in creating and maintaining interest as well as helping the audience understand.

This assumes, of course, that the aids are well chosen or well prepared and effectively used. The presenter should know the types of aids that are helpful and the best way to use them. The most frequently used aids are flipcharts, overhead transparencies, Microsoft PowerPoint presentations, and handouts.

Effective Aid Characteristics

The leader should remember that an aid is just that, something to help make the presentation effective. It should meet the following criteria:

- pertinent to the subject being presented
- easy to read or hear by everyone in the audience
- simple enough to be understood without a lot of detailed explanation.

Some other characteristics that are not absolutely necessary but might help maintain interest and create understanding are

- attractive (perhaps colorful)
- creative
- humorous (and still pertinent)
- varied (using different types to add variety and interest).

Effective Aid Uses

The aid should be used to help the leader make the presentation effective. Therefore, the right aid should be selected or prepared for the right spot in the presentation. The leader should consider, "Where will an aid help me communicate and/or get attention?"

In using the aid, planning and preparation should ensure that the equipment is set up and works properly. Also, whoever is using the aid must be prepared and qualified—in other words, know how to use it and correct any problems that might occur. For example, Microsoft PowerPoint has many possibilities for problems. If you use it, practice ahead of time and be sure that any handouts that go with it are synchronized with your presentation.

After the aid has been used, the leader should do whatever is most appropriate. Possible actions are

- Dispose of the visual aid because it has served its purpose and might prove to be a distraction.
- Leave the visual aid in front of the audience so that the leader can refer to it in making other points or in summarizing.

Effective Presentation Skills

Here are some specific suggestions for the three parts of a presentation:

Introduction

- Welcome the group. A few introductory comments will warm up the group and gain their attention. For this reason, humor is often used in opening a lecture session.
- State the subject matter of the presentation, and explain how and why it was selected.
- State the objectives of the presentation: What is to be accomplished, and what should the participants gain from it.
- Explain how the presentation and the achievement of the objectives will benefit the participants.
- Provide a brief preview of the presentation; describe the points you'll be covering and their importance to the participants.

Body

This is the heart of the meeting. Plan how best to get the points across to your audience. Consider the finer points that make the distinction between a boring bunch of words and an exciting presentation.

To further help you catch and keep the interest of your participants, here are some tips for making a presentation:

- Use clear and simple language.
- Use language understood by the whole group. Use terms drawn from their own work situations.
- Be specific. Your examples should always relate exactly and directly to the point being made.
- Use aids effectively.

Using an Outline: It's not difficult to make your notes complete enough to include all the illustrative examples you will need to build on the main points. And using notes, instead of reading a text, gives your audience more of a sense of being spoken to directly and less a sense that they are simply being stuffed with boring information. And if you read from a text, you have to keep your eyes on the paper. Speaking from notes, you can have eye contact with the people all over the room and show them that you're talking to them, not at them. And this helps maintain their interest and attention.

Using Aids Effectively: The speaker's use of aids can have a considerable effect on the audience. Used well, they will imprint the point on the mind of each person in the group. They will also add that all-important touch of showmanship to the meeting. Used poorly, aids can slow down the speaker and detract from the message.

The four aids most frequently used are

1. flipcharts
   - Print large enough so the entire audience can easily read it.
   - Keep it simple. Use only key words.
   - Know what is to be written before starting to write so you can get everything to look well balanced.
   - Stand sideways while writing.
   - Use color, arrows, underscores, circles, etc., for emphasis.
   - Use a new page to start a new idea.

2. overhead projector transparencies
   - Make sure each is clear and uncluttered.
   - Use color.
   - Use creativity, such as pictures or charts instead of just words.
   - Reveal one line at a time when presenting so the participants can't read ahead.
   - Give the participants blanks to complete to make them think.
   - Don't dwell too long on one transparency.

3. Microsoft PowerPoint presentations
   - Don't spend too much time giving background data on your organization.
   - Don't put too much material on one slide.
   - Use colors that will show up clearly—avoid light colors.
   - Use creativity on the slides—don't make them boring by just giving details.
   - Allow room on participant handouts of the slides for taking notes.
   - Don't simply say what is on the handouts.

4. handouts
   - Be sure everyone has a copy.
   - Number the pages if there are more than three pages.
   - Don't fill in all the information. Allow room on each page for taking notes.

A summary and more details on the overhead projector, Microsoft PowerPoint presentation, and handouts are included in chapter 10.

Conclusion
   - Complete the presentation with a review of the main points, emphasizing the importance of understanding and remembering the information.
   - Include any comments that are designed to get the participants to apply what they learned.
   - Suggest reference materials or sources of additional information for those who may be interested.

An effective presentation requires adequate preparation. The amount of time it takes to prepare varies widely and depends on such factors as the amount of material that must be found or learned, the length of the presentation, previous speaking experience, type and number of audiovisual aids to be used, and previous knowledge of the audience.

An effective presentation also requires skill in the presentation itself. This skill can be learned and developed. Some leaders are blessed with certain personality characteristics that make them especially effective. Some of these qualities can't be learned. Therefore, some presenters can never reach the level of effectiveness that others reach. Courses in effective speaking can help because they provide opportunities for practice and constructive critique. The reading of appropriate books (such as this) can also help because they provide practical suggestions.

Finally, the use of audiovisual aids can help to create and maintain the interest of the audience. These aids can also serve as a catalyst to persuade the participants to act. And the very process of seeing as well as hearing will help them remember. Use as much audiovisual equipment as practical. Check and recheck all equipment after it is set up in the meeting room. Nothing kills a meeting like a public address system or a projector that won't work. Rehearse presentations with the equipment operator, especially when using Microsoft PowerPoint.

Chapter 8

How to Get and Maintain Enthusiastic Involvement

If the meeting is going to be productive, enthusiastic involvement is necessary. Involvement need not be active talking; it can be active listening. It can also be enthusiastic participation in an activity or problem that is given to the participants. It means the speaker has the undivided interest and attention of the participants. It also includes a commitment to help accomplish the objectives of the meeting.

Initial Enthusiasm

The first requirement for enthusiastic involvement is to get participants to want to come to the meeting. Their initial attitude toward being there is critical. To build this initial enthusiasm, the leader must convince each participant that there is a need for the meeting and the participant should be there. This can be done personally or by means of a well-planned notice that is sent to the participants.

The second requirement for initial enthusiasm is to schedule the meeting at a time that participants feel is the best time for the meeting. Often, this requires the leader to check potential times with participants before deciding on the final time. Also, the right amount of advance notice must be given to participants so they can plan to be there without having mental or physical interruptions.

Do—
Give plenty of advance notice as to the date and place of meeting.

The third requirement for building initial enthusiasm is to select a place that participants feel is the best place for the meeting. Two important factors are

1. proximity to the workplace of the participants (Sometimes it is best to hold the meeting as close as possible to the workplace so that it will require minimum travel time. At other times, it is better to get away from the workplace to avoid mental and physical interruptions in the meeting. In general, the shorter the meeting, the closer it should be to the workplace. This presupposes, of course, that adequate facilities are available.)

2. physical facilities. (Minimum requirements are the right size room [not too large and especially not too small], the right temperature, comfortable furniture, quiet and free from interruptions and distractions, and free from posts or other obstructions that prevent participants from seeing the leader and the aids.)

> **Do—**
> Maintain a fast-moving, varied program with adequate time for two-way discussion.

The fourth requirement for getting initial enthusiasm is the personal enthusiasm of the leader. This requirement is very important.

Continued Enthusiasm

Once the meeting begins, the leader's challenge is to maintain the enthusiasm. Below are 11 factors that reduce initial enthusiasm that should be avoided during a meeting:

1. **The leader is not prepared**. It doesn't take the participants long to know whether the leader is prepared and ready to go.
2. **The meeting doesn't start on time**. This is one of the most frustrating experiences of busy people who recognize the value of time.
3. **The leader gets the meeting off to a slow start**. This could be a long story that falls flat, an audiovisual aid that doesn't work, or a poor introduction by the leader.
4. **The objectives seem unimportant to the participants**. The participants will immediately evaluate the objectives in terms of the time and energy they will expend.
5. **The objectives are unclear to the participants**. Confused participants will quickly lose enthusiasm.
6. **The leader reads too much material**. Most participants are readily turned off by a leader who reads for more than a few minutes.

7. **The meeting gets out of control**. Examples: Participants make a comment or ask a question that is off topic, side conversation takes place between two participants, two or more participants argue with each other, one or two participants dominate the meeting, or the leader gets off the subject.

8. **The leader dominates the meeting**. In most meetings, some participants want to express themselves and their opinions on the topic.

9. **The meeting runs too long without a break**. Remember that the mind can absorb only as much as the seat can stand.

10. **There is no variety or change of pace**. Don't let the participants get bored.

> **Do—**
> Change the pace of the meeting every day; insist on program variety.

11. **The leader lacks personal enthusiasm**. Set an example for the group—get enthusiastic! Keep it going throughout the entire meeting so that the participants will follow your example.

These 11 factors tend to dampen enthusiasm. Therefore, their opposites will help maintain the participants' enthusiasm throughout the meeting.

How to Maintain Enthusiasm Throughout the Meeting

1. **Be prepared.** Do all the things described in chapter 4.
2. **Start the meeting on time.** Do this even if all the participants aren't there. Build a reputation of starting meetings on time, and participants will be there.
3. **Have a good introduction.** Get the attention of the group.
4. **Convince the participants that the meeting is important.** Make them realize that their time is being well spent.
5. **Communicate the objectives clearly.** If the objectives are clear to the leader, there is no excuse for having them unclear to participants.
6. **Don't read any more than necessary.** Use notes and talk to the participants. Maintain good eye contact.
7. **Maintain control.** Use the techniques described in chapter 9.
8. **Play the appropriate role.** Use the approaches and methods described in chapter 5.
9. **Take necessary breaks.** Take into account the comfort of the chairs and the nature of the subject. Be alert to any uneasiness or restlessness on the part of the participants. A good rule of thumb is to have a break at least every 90 minutes. Obviously, the nature of the subject would be a factor. If the subject content is heavy and technical, a break every hour is probably important.
10. **Use variety.** Variety in approach and method should accomplish two things: get attention and help accomplish the objectives. Occasionally, a short story or aid may be used just to get attention, even though it has nothing to do with the objective.
11. **Maintain your own enthusiasm as the leader.** The group will follow your example.

Final Enthusiasm

The conclusion of the meeting should find participants with the same enthusiasm they had when the meeting started. Leaders should aim for participants to take away five conclusions after the meeting:

1. Participants should leave the meeting with the thought, "That was an excellent meeting." (all meetings)
2. Participants should go back to their jobs with enthusiasm to apply what they learned. (instructional meeting)
3. Participants should go back to their jobs with enthusiasm to implement the solution. (problem-solving meetings)
4. Participants should leave the meeting with enthusiasm to attend the next meeting. (all meetings)
5. Participants should leave the meeting with a strong feeling of contribution. (information-getting, problem-solving, and possibly instructional meetings)

Don't—
Forget to outline the action you expect as a result of the meeting.

Any or all of these can be accomplished by a leader who conducts a productive meeting. They are also directly related to the conclusion of the meeting, which is described in detail in chapter 9.

The following quote from Henry Ford emphasizes the need for the personal enthusiasm of the leader:

"You can do anything if you have enthusiasm. It is the yeast that makes your hope rise to the stars, it is the sparkle in your eye, it is the swing in your gait, the grip of your hand, the irresistible surge of your will, and your energy to execute your ideas. Enthusiasm is at the bottom of all progress. With it there is accomplishment; without it there are only alibis."

Chapter 9

How to Control
and Conclude a Meeting

═══ ➤

How to Control a Meeting

Regardless of the type of meeting, the leader must control it if it's going to be productive. *Control* means to keep it moving so that objectives are accomplished in minimum time with satisfied participants. The last phrase of this definition (with satisfied participants) clearly indicates that control is an art, not a science.

The best way to control a meeting is to prevent it from getting out of control. Good planning and preparation by the leader are essential. Other factors that prevent loss of control are a clear statement of objectives, clear questions and instructions during the meeting, and a high level of interest and enthusiasm on the part of the participants.

Some leaders feel that the best way to control a meeting is to prevent any kind of group involvement or participation. This leader does not ask any questions of the group and does not allow participants to ask questions. This kind of control might be too tight. It might accomplish meeting objectives in minimum time but might create dissatisfaction among participants who leave the meeting saying, "I don't agree with what the leader said, but I didn't have an opportunity to speak."

> **Do—**
> Take time to listen; encourage discussion.

The effective leader controls by preventing the meeting from getting out of control but still provides the climate for free expression on the part of the participants. If the meeting starts to get out of control, the effective leader brings it under control quickly and tactfully.

Loss of control can take many forms. Table 9-1 lists some of the more common situations and the probable causes.

Table 9-1. Loss of Control.

What Happens?	Why?
1. Participant makes a comment or asks a question that is off the topic.	A. Objective or topic being discussed is not clear to the participant. B. Participant unintentionally gets off the topic because of a pressing problem or need.
2. Side conversation takes place between two participants.	A. Something in the meeting stimulated the participants to talk to each other. (Their conversation may be right on the subject.) B. They are bored or disinterested and their conversation is off the topic.
3. Participants are distracted.	A. The distraction is a major one, and all participants are distracted even though they are very interested in the meeting. B. Participants are distracted because of their lack of interest in the meeting.
4. Two or more participants argue with each other.	A. Participants are stimulated by the subject and are expressing their feelings and opinions on the topic. B. Participants are using the meeting as a vehicle to vent their feelings and emotions toward each other.
5. One or two participants dominate the meeting.	A. Some participants are quick thinkers who express themselves easily and are trying to help the leader accomplish the objectives. (They may be on or off the topic.) B. Participants are trying to gain attention from the leader or the group.
6. Participants get nervous and are anxious to leave.	A. The meeting is running past the scheduled time. B. The meeting has become nonproductive, and participants feel they are wasting their time. C. Participants have other commitments.
7. Participants refuse to participate.	A. Participants are uninterested in the meeting. B. Participants are afraid to participate because the meeting climate is not right. C. Participants don't like the leader or the way the leader has ridiculed one or more participants.
8. Leader gets off the topic.	A. The leader is not well prepared and inadvertently goes off on a tangent. B. A participant asks a question or makes a comment that takes the leader off the topic.

Below is an examination of each one of the eight common situations and a suggestion of what a leader can do to prevent loss of control or to handle it if it occurs:

- **Problem 1: Participant makes a comment or asks a question that is off the topic.**

  Prevent: Be sure that the objective or subject being discussed is clear to all participants. Objectives and questions that the leader asks of the participants should be carefully prepared in advance. The leader should write the objective on a whiteboard or flipchart before or during the meeting. If the leader is asking a question, he or she should ask the question orally and then write it on a flipchart. This accomplishes two things. First, it clarifies the question because the participants see as well as hear it. Second, it gives participants a chance to think about their answers and increases the probability that more of the participants will be able to answer. The pause while the leader writes the question is not an embarrassing pause.

  Handle: The leader must handle this problem to the satisfaction of the participant as well as the others in the group. The first requirement is for the leader to recognize what is happening. Some leaders are so happy to get participants that they aren't cognizant that the participant is off the topic. The second requirement is to handle the situation in such a way that the participant doesn't resent what the leader does. Therefore, tact is important. Here are some suggested approaches:

  — The leader apologizes to the group with such words as, "I guess I haven't made the objective (or question) clear. Let me state it again."
  — The leader tactfully asks the participant, "How does your comment (or question) tie in with the subject we are discussing?"
  — The leader tactfully sidesteps the comment or question with such words as, "That's a good comment (or question), but it's a little off the topic. I wonder if I could see you after the meeting to discuss it."

- **Problem 2: Side conversation takes place between two participants.**

  Prevent: Be sure the objective and subject being discussed are clear to all participants. Also, be sure the meeting is both interesting and beneficial to maintain the attention of all participants.

Do—
Keep the meeting purpose and objectives clear in everyone's mind.

Handle: If a side conversation develops, the leader should assume that it's on the subject. Even if it is an incorrect assumption, give the benefit of the doubt to the participants and, thereby, maintain their positive attitudes. Here are some possible approaches:

— Pause for a few seconds without calling particular attention to them. The silence may cut short their conversation. Look at your notes or do something similar that implies that the pause is for your benefit. If appropriate, take a short break because the side conversation may indicate restlessness on the part of the participants.

— Ask them directly if they would like to share their ideas with the group. The manner in which you do it should clearly indicate your assumption that they are discussing the subject of the meeting.

● Problem 3: Participants are distracted.

Do—
Allow time for recreation if the meeting lasts several days.

Prevent: Keep the meeting so interesting and productive that participants are not easily distracted. People who are deeply absorbed in a subject or activity are usually oblivious to any distractions that occur. Sometimes distractions can be prevented if the meeting is held at the proper place and the proper time. The planning of the leader should include how to avoid distractions and interruptions.

Handle: If all or nearly all of the participants are distracted, then stop the meeting and recognize the distraction. Don't try to compete with it. Perhaps a break is in order to let people look at the distraction (such as an ambulance or police siren) and discuss it. Even though it takes time, the leader would be nonproductive in trying to keep the meeting going.

If a small minority of the group is distracted, the leader may choose to ignore it and continue with the meeting. It might be a good spot for an example or story that isn't important to the success of the meeting. Or it may be a good place to summarize what has happened so far.

Do—
Use imagination and creativity to make points.

● Problem 4: Two or more participants argue with each other.

Prevent: Clarify objectives and topics under discussion so off-topic arguing does not take place. To prevent on-the-subject arguing, the leader can quote Peter Drucker who states, "It's not who is right, but what is right that is important." The leader can then state, "We want the opinions from each one of you. Say what you think. But also be willing to listen to and consider the ideas of others. Let's control our emotions."

Handle: The leader can use the Peter Drucker quote, "It's not who is right, but what is right that is important" and then concentrate on the thoughts presented and not the people who presented them. Also, the leader can say something like, "Hold it a minute. Let's see what the rest of the group thinks."

Or, the leader can stop the meeting and call attention to the objectives and the need to move toward accomplishing them. The important thing is to regain control of the meeting without alienating either of the arguers. If the argument is on the subject, the leader should either take a stand or call on the other participants for opinions or facts. If the argument is off the topic, the leader should restate the objective or topic being discussed.

Don't—
Allow gripe sessions to develop.

- **Problem 5: One or two participants dominate the meeting.**

Prevent: If the problem can be anticipated, the leader should start the meeting by encouraging all to participate. If the leader knows a particular person who might dominate, the leader can contact the person prior to the meeting and suggest restraint in participation so that others can participate. Calling on people by name instead of asking for volunteers can also prevent the domination by an individual. If the leader is going to call on people to participate, the leader should be sure that the person can answer the question. One of the ways to do this is to ask all participants to write down their answers to a question. For example, a leader might ask, "What ideas do you have for improving quality? Will each person please write down a few ideas that come to mind?" Then, the leader can call on almost anybody to answer the question and avoid those who tend to dominate. In all cases, the leader should give the name of the person before asking the question.

Handle: The leader should handle the problem without embarrassing the enthusiastic participant. Here are some possible approaches:

— Tactfully interrupt with a statement like, "I think we get your point, Mabel; now let's see what Harriet has to say."

— Move around the room and purposely but subtly turn your back on this person so you don't see the hand raised and, thereby, discourage participation.

— Give the person a specific job to do. For example, "Tom, I wonder if you'll come up to the flipchart and record the ideas from the group."

— Interrupt the person with, "Bill, I hate to interrupt you, but time is running short, and I'd like to get the thoughts of the other people."

● **Problem 6: Participants get nervous and are anxious to leave.**

Prevent: Perhaps you set a closing time for the meeting and you aren't going to make it. Next time, either conclude the meeting on time or don't set a closing time. Instead, inform the group that "the meeting will probably be over about 3:30 (give yourself plenty of time), but we are going to stay until we solve the problem."

Perhaps you picked a bad time for the meeting and the participants have more important (to them) things to do. Be sure to schedule meetings when people are free of pressures to do other things.

Perhaps they are anxious to leave because they feel they are wasting their time. In other words, they are dissatisfied with the meeting. Next time, be sure you plan and run a productive meeting.

Handle: When the participants become restless, do something to prevent a disaster. Here are some possibilities:

— Do something to renew their interest in the meeting. A dramatic story, a project for them to do, or a question to stimulate attention and interest are possible techniques.

— Conclude the meeting, and set a time for the next meeting.

— Give them a break (perhaps they have been sitting too long). If possible, give them refreshments to help renew their enthusiasm.

Do—
Provide an interesting, but businesslike, meeting.

● **Problem 7: Participants refuse to participate.**

Prevent: Be sure the meeting climate encourages participation. Also, do not alienate or embarrass those who do participate. Finally, keep the meeting interesting and productive so that the participants know what's going on and are attentive and concerned.

Handle: Obviously, the approach depends on the reason why participants won't participate. If the problem is disinterest or boredom, the leader must get the participants' interest and attention. The leader can then call on people by name if he or she is sure they can answer the question. In preparation for this, the leader can ask each person to write down the answer to the question.

If the reason for nonparticipation is fear of embarrassment or ridicule, the leader must carefully eliminate that fear by such statements as, "Don't be afraid to speak up even if you disagree with me" or "Don't hesitate to ask a question even if you aren't sure it's a good question." Another approach is to quickly form buzz groups and ask three to six people to formulate a question or give an answer. Groups are usually eager to have a spokesperson report for them. And the spokesperson is not afraid because he or she speaks for the group and not for himself or herself.

To encourage further participation, the leader must be very careful not to embarrass or ridicule those who do participate, even if the comment is foolish, off the topic, or derogatory. The toughest problem to handle is when the group is hostile to the leader. Encouraging participants to speak up probably won't help. It might be possible to form buzz groups and give them a specific assignment. The other possibility is to move to another subject and get them so attentive and absorbed that they will forget their hostility.

> **Don't—**
> Single anyone out for criticism.

- **Problem 8: Leader gets off the topic.**

Prevent: Don't get off the topic. First of all the leader must be well prepared and clear on objectives as well as on the approach to be used to accomplish the objectives. Questions to be asked and information to be presented by the leader should be planned to prevent getting off the subject.

Usually the leader is drawn off the subject by a comment or question from a participant. The leader must be alert to this possibility. Many leaders are so anxious to get a question from a participant that they become anxious to answer it and don't even realize that the question and the answer are off the subject. To prevent being drawn off the subject, the leader should quickly evaluate each comment and question that comes from participants. If it is not on the topic, the leader should call attention to that fact and postpone discussion until an appropriate time, during or after the meeting.

Handle: If the leader realizes he or she is off the subject, an apology is in order, such as, "I'm afraid I got carried away and got off the subject. I wish we had time to continue, but we have an objective to accomplish, and the other subject will have to wait for an appropriate time." Even if the leader was drawn off the topic by an irrelevant question from a participant, the leader should take the blame. If a participant notices that the leader is off the topic, the participant should tactfully but firmly call it to the attention of the leader. (For more details, see Appendix C.)

Don't—
Present extraneous subjects that stray from the theme of the meeting.

The most difficult aspect of conducting productive meetings is control. It will require knowledge of control approaches, quick thinking, and a lot of tact. The best way to control a meeting is to prevent it from getting out of control. This can be done by careful preparation by the leader, including the anticipation of events that might happen to cause the meeting to get out of control. For example, if the leader thinks that one participant may dominate to the detriment of the meeting effectiveness, the leader can talk to the participant before the meeting and possibly prevent the domination from taking place. Regardless of the preparation, however, the leader will be challenged with situations that require control procedures to be taken during the meeting. Being alert to these possibilities is half the battle. The other half is to take the proper corrective action if the situation does occur.

How to Conclude a Meeting

It is just as important to conclude a meeting effectively as it is to have a good introduction. The conclusion of the meeting must maintain the enthusiasm that the participants have experienced up to that point. Each one should leave with the attitude, "I'm glad I came!"

There are a variety of ways to conclude a meeting and accomplish the final enthusiasm objective. Some leaders like to tell a story that may be related to the objectives of the meeting. If it's a funny story effectively told, it may well send people away with a smile or a laugh. However, the conclusion of a meeting should do more than that. It should send people away with a feeling of satisfaction that their time and energy were well spent. Depending on the type of meeting, it could give them a feeling of accomplishment and achievement. It could also give them a good feeling of contribution. Or it could give them a feeling of importance.

Table 9-2 shows a few simple do's and one don't that apply to the conclusion of most meetings.

Table 9-3 offers a little quiz to see how you feel about concluding a meeting. Agree or disagree with each statement, and read my answers and the rationale for them.

Do—
End the meeting on a high note.

Table 9-2. Concluding a Meeting Do's and Don'ts

Do

1. Restate the objective of the meeting.
2. Summarize what was accomplished.
3. Thank participants for their contribution. (problem-solving, information-getting, and instructional meetings)
4. Thank participants for coming and for their attention and interest. (information-giving and instructional meetings)
5. Thank participants for their participation.
6. Give assignments to one or more participants.
7. Tell participants the time, place, and objectives of the next meeting.
8. Give final announcements, such as, "Minutes of the meeting will be sent out in 10 days" or "Our next meeting will be held two weeks from today at the same time" or "Remember to tell your subordinates what we discussed today."

Don't

Don't end the meeting with "We have time for just one more question."

In the first place, the leader doesn't have any idea what to expect when a meeting is ended with "We have time for just one more question." It might be a question that is related or unrelated to the objective. It might be a question that is peculiar to the person who asked it or of general interest. The question may take five seconds or one minute to ask, perhaps with several parts. And a good answer might take one word, or it might take a lengthy explanation to answer. All of these unpredictables clearly say, "Don't do it!" And besides, everyone else is eager to go!

A more important reason not to end a meeting with this phrase is that there is a good way to end the meeting. The most important is that the meeting should conclude with a summary of the objectives and the accomplishments.

There is nothing wrong with a question-and-answer period. The point is, don't end the meeting that way.

Table 9-3. What is the Proper Way to Conclude a Meeting?

Agree	Disagree	
☐	☐	1. When a mixture of about 50/50 between participation and presentation has been reached, conclude the meeting.
☐	☐	2. A quick check of your meeting plan will clue you as to whether you should continue or end the meeting.
☐	☐	3. Forget about the clock. Most conferees don't want to go until everything is settled.
☐	☐	4. Never break up a meeting in the middle. It's bad to schedule a follow-up session to complete the subject because everyone will be cold to the idea.
☐	☐	5. Warn the group when it's near the closing time, and let them know you have time for a couple more questions.
☐	☐	6. Take the group temperature with a question like, "Would you like to dig deeper into the subject?" This will clue you as to when they've had enough and when you can close it off.
☐	☐	7. The conference leader is responsible for guiding the group to a proper conclusion.
☐	☐	8. The pressure of time sometimes makes it difficult to get all the ideas of everyone, but with proper planning and effective control, you can achieve this objective in the time available.
☐	☐	9. Keep the meeting going as long as you feel the results are worthwhile, the conferees are interested, and the clock and the meeting plan permit.

Below are my answers and explanations to the quiz in table 9-3.

Statement	Correct Answer	Discussion
1	Disagree	Just having a 50/50 mixture of participation and presentation is not enough of a reason for ending the meeting.
2	Agree	Every leader should have a plan. The plan is the guide. If you completed the plan, end the meeting.
3	Disagree	Most conferees are watching the clock closer than you are. If time has run out, end the meeting or possibly poll the group to get their reaction if you need a few more minutes to reach the planned conclusion.
4	Disagree	Sometimes it's a good idea to schedule a follow-up session if you have not reached your objective. If you do, it is important to convince the group that a proper conclusion is necessary.

Statement	Correct Answer	Discussion
5	Disagree	Don't make the mistake of ending a meeting by saying, "We have time for one (or a couple) more questions." If someone did ask an involved question at this stage, you may find it difficult to end on time. And a summary is the proper way to end it.
6	Disagree	The completion of your plan should determine when you end the meeting, not necessarily a consensus of the group.
7	Agree	This is definitely your responsibility, and few people do it well. It takes practice. Remember to summarize and try to reach the proper conclusion.
8	Agree	Many times the pressure of time will limit discussion. Don't let this bother you. Just make the fact known as to why you must limit discussion to end on time.
9	Agree/Disagree	This is good criteria, but the end of the meeting should come when you have reached your objectives, even when you complete the meeting ahead of schedule. Practically no one will object to your ending the meeting ahead of schedule.

Chapter 10

How to Conduct a Productive Training Meeting

Most of the principles and approaches that are described in this book are pertinent to all types of meetings, including training and departmental. The following chapters are critical in regard to making them productive:

- Chapter 4 provides details on how to prepare for a meeting.
- Chapter 5 describes the role of the leader.
- Chapter 6 describes using questions to stimulate discussion.
- Chapter 7 describes principles and techniques for presenting information effectively.

These four chapters should be studied before reading this one. On the average, a training meeting should have about a 50/50 participation ratio between leader and participants. This will vary a great deal depending on the content and the knowledge and experience of the participants. But it does illustrate the fact that the leader must be a trainer to present information effectively and a facilitator to conduct guided participation.

The Participants

The size and composition of the trainees should be considered because they are critical factors that relate to participation. For example, a large group usually limits the kind of participative approaches that can be used. Likewise, a group of inexperienced trainees tends to reduce the opportunities for participation. Therefore, care should be taken to determine the composition and size of the group that will be instructed. When this has been done, the approaches and methods can be selected.

It is generally agreed that the size of a class in supervisory training should not exceed 30. In many companies, group size is limited to less than 20. The optimum size of the group depends on objectives, room size, and the skill of the instructors.

As to the composition of the group, it is generally felt that the participants should be at the same level in the organization. For example, supervisory training meetings should be limited to first-level supervisors, and higher-level managers should not be in attendance. However, some companies have taken a different approach and have purposely included several levels of management. One particular organization, for example, frequently conducts sessions in which it has family groups, groups in which several levels of management from the same department are in attendance at the same time. If the attendance of higher-level management people in supervisory training meetings inhibits the participation and learning that is taking place, restrict the attendance to first-level supervisors. However, if the presence of higher-level management people enhances the involvement and learning of supervisors, then several levels of management should be included.

Another consideration regarding composition of the group is whether a meeting should be attended by all supervisors and foremen or only by those who need the subject matter to be discussed. As a general rule, most companies do not single out those who need it most. They include all supervisors and foremen in the meeting so that no stigma is attached to those in attendance. They also do it because those who are better supervisors and do not need the subject content can help the others learn. Basic supervisory programs should be compulsory for all supervisors to attend. Select programs can be limited to those who need it most or those who want to attend.

Introduction

This is a very critical phase for a productive meeting. The example on the next page will provide some suggestions.

Presentation vs. Participation

The mix is on a continuum, running from total presentation to total participation (see figure 5-1). One controlling factor is how much the participants know about the subject. This implies that the meeting leader ordinarily should know how much the group knows about the subject. Some of this information may be learned during the meeting.

Example

You are the new manager. Even though there may be those, especially subordinates, who feel they should have gotten the job, you were appointed by higher management, and you must accept the responsibility that goes with your new job.

You know what you want to accomplish in this meeting and what commitment you made to your manager. You have agreed to these broad objectives:

- Raise revenues to meet the present company averages for other similar divisions.
- Raise the level of the measured services up to the 97-98 range.
- Select and promote women and other minority employees to fulfill the affirmative action goals and timetables.
- Reduce absenteeism to an agreed-on level without denying your people their rights under the benefit plan.

With these objectives in mind, plus the fact that you are new and a stranger to some of your subordinates, plan your opening statements. Make some notes on just what you intend to say and do. You do not need complete sentences, just brief notes you can use in presenting your ideas.

Think in terms of:

- setting a proper climate for your meeting
- introducing yourself
- informing them of your commitments
- informing them of your desire for their help in setting and reaching specific objectives for their own departments. (Consider telling them that you will meet with each one at a later date.)

Ten ideas for opening the meeting:

1. Have a plan for introducing yourself to those who don't know you and vice versa.
2. Tell the group your reasons for having the meeting.
3. Clarify the objectives of the meeting so that the group will concentrate on the topic and not go off in unrelated directions.
4. Tell them your plan for presentation and participation.
5. Give them an opportunity to present their own comments and suggestions.
6. Make it clear that you will consider their input when making decisions.
7. Make it clear that you cannot accomplish your objectives without help from every member of the team.
8. Make it clear that your intent is to outline the broad objectives for the division in this meeting and that each person will have an opportunity to help set his or her own specific objectives on a one-to-one basis later.
9. Make it clear that while you did agree to division objectives, your mind is not closed. You are willing to listen to everyone's suggestions.
10. Make it clear that you feel that the objectives set by upper management are reasonable and necessary and can be attained by a team that is willing to accept the challenges.

Once the group is assembled and you are the leader, you need to control the mix. This requires two skills: presentation (your role as a trainer) and participation (your role as a facilitator).

Classroom Techniques

In selecting the best methods and techniques for teaching, keep in mind that the meeting should be enjoyable as well as beneficial because you want to send the participants back to their departments feeling satisfied with the meeting. My son, Jim, and I have adopted the PIE approach to teaching—Practical, Interactive, and Enjoyable—for all of our teaching. You may want to adopt the same philosophy!

Do—
Give it your all; if an event is worth doing, it is worth doing well.

The first consideration for using any technique is to be sure it helps accomplish the objectives that have been set. There are many techniques and methods that can be used to meet objectives. Participants will enjoy some more than others. Therefore, techniques should be used that accomplish the objectives as well as make the sessions interesting and enjoyable to the participants. Participants who enjoy the sessions will probably pay more attention and, thereby, learn more. This section will discuss some of the techniques that can contribute to the enjoyment as well as the productivity of meetings.

Guided Participation

Guided participation is a common technique for use in conducting instructional meetings. It consists of participation on the part of the learners under the guidance and control of the leaders. This is where the trainer becomes a facilitator. It can be most effectively used when experienced participants have ideas to contribute.

Do—
Promote discussion topics in advance, and allow each person time to give opinions.

There are two basic approaches to guided participation. The most common form is to have open discussion in which the leader gives a question or problem to the entire group. Volunteers answer it, and discussion proceeds.

The other approach is to divide the group into buzz groups of four to six people so that each person can participate more actively. Each buzz group is given a topic to discuss or a problem to solve. A case study is frequently used. Each buzz group may be given the same topic or a different one.

Using Buzz Groups Effectively

For buzz groups to be effective, the following guidelines should be observed:

- Before the question or problem is assigned, a chairperson should be selected for each buzz group. This can be done by a variety of means. The group can select its own chairperson by pointing fingers or other democratic processes. Other approaches can be used to add variety and enjoyment to the meeting. For example, the following criteria might be used:
  a. the person with the brightest clothes
  b. the person with the nearest birthday
  c. the person who lives the farthest away
  d. the person with the most children
  e. the person with the most (or least) company experience.

- The chairperson should clearly understand what he or she has to do, including
  a. get everyone to participate
  b. contribute own ideas
  c. control the meeting
  d. reach the objective.

- A secretary should be appointed by the chairperson to take notes.
- The instructions to the buzz groups must be clear in:
  a. exactly what the participants are supposed to do
  b. how much time the participants have
  c. what will happen after the buzz groups finish (e.g., reports from each one, role playing).

NOTE: This aspect of buzz groups cannot be overemphasized. The leader must be sure that the buzz groups do not start out with a very common statement, "What are we supposed to do?"

There are many assignments that can be given to buzz groups, including the following that relate to the presentation by the instructor:

- Team 1: What was the most important point that the presentation made?
- Team 2: What point was made that you want to challenge?
- Team 3: What point would you like clarified or expanded?
- Team 4: What point was left out that you'd like to add?

In this example, each buzz group would be given a specific assignment that requires each person to listen to the entire presentation. It also provides a good basis for practical discussion within each team. When each group reports, the buzz group provides a good analysis and summary of the various aspects of the presentation for the entire group. Therefore, this approach provides high motivation to listen as well as worthwhile classroom involvement.

Aids

The two purposes of aids are to help make the presentation effective and to get and maintain interest and attention. Every time a leader shows a new visual aid, there is immediate attention from the participants. The length of that interest depends on what happens next.

The most common aids used by effective trainers are flipcharts, overhead projector transparencies, Microsoft PowerPoint slides, and handouts. In departmental meetings, the flipchart or the whiteboard is the most frequently used aid. In training meetings, Microsoft PowerPoint slides are used most frequently. Sometimes handouts of each slide are given to the participants so they can add notes or just have a copy to take back to their organization. Some national conferences give no handouts, but the participants receive a CD of the slides, usually in advance of the conference so participants can print them out if they wish. This is frustrating to most participants and presenters, but it is a cost saver for the organization that runs the conference.

> **Do—**
> Use visuals—
> slides, movies,
> etc.—and keep
> them short.
> Change these daily.

Even at national conferences I still use overhead projector transparencies along with handouts and a flipchart. I have better contact with the group that way and have great opportunities to reveal one line at a time to build interest and get audience involvement. There is a new projector that will project both overhead transparencies and typed material. It projects from the bottom (overhead transparencies) and from the top (printed material). It sounds like a great invention, but it distorts the colored transparencies. If you use transparencies, request not to have the new overhead projector.

Case Studies

The words *case study* are used by people to mean different things. Some people think of a case study as a detailed description of an industrial or business situation. To use this type of case study would require a great deal of advance reading and study by participants and a great deal of time to discuss it and benefit from its use. An alternative approach would be to find or write a short case study (not more than one page) describing a particular situation that is important for the group to discuss. Some case studies are presented on film instead of on paper. Usually, dramatized case studies on film are more effective than written case studies because the participants can see and feel the situation better.

Here are a few tips for using aids:

- Be sure everyone can see and read them.
- Don't put too much on one page.
- Remove them as soon as you are finished with them so they won't be a distraction.
- Don't remove them if you aren't finished with them and want the audience to see them. (For example, if you put the objectives of a meeting on a flipchart, leave them in front during the entire meeting so participants will be constantly reminded to stay on the subject.)
- Be sure everyone has the handouts and at the proper time. (If there is a room monitor for your session, be sure that the monitor is ready to pass out the handouts when the early participants come in. Be sure to arrange for this ahead of time. And be sure there are enough handouts for everyone.)
- Ask questions orally, and write them on a flipchart. (This will give the participants time to understand the question and consider if they will answer it and what they will say. Otherwise, there will probably be an awkward silence while participants consider the question and if and how they will answer it. See chapter 6 for more details on the proper use of questions.)
- Reveal one line or chart at a time when using the overhead projector or Microsoft PowerPoint. (When presenters use Microsoft PowerPoint presentations, most of the presenters show a slide that has many points. Participants are apt to read ahead and not listen to what the presenter is saying.)

One case would be assigned to each subgroup in the meeting. This can be done either by asking each person to volunteer to participate in the case in which the person is most interested or by assigning one case to each table or buzz group. Each group would then be given the following assignment:

- Select a chairperson who is responsible for leading and controlling the discussion and reaching the objectives.
- Appoint a secretary who is responsible for taking notes and summarizing the discussion that takes place.
- Complete the following objectives:
  - Discuss and agree on how employees in your department would react to the specific change described in your case.
  - Discuss and decide how you would communicate the change to the people in your department.
  - Discuss and decide how you would see that the change is effectively implemented in your department.

Following are examples of four written case studies that could be used in a training meeting for supervisors on how to manage change effectively. They are all related to a line production department. Similar cases can be written for technical and professional supervisors.

1. The Case of the New Equipment

You are foreman of a machine shop.

To reduce costs and meet competition, you need to install automatic equipment to replace some of the manual operations in your department. You have looked at new equipment and are still considering two machines. You have not yet decided which one to buy.

Your department now consists of 15 hourly workers. When the new equipment is in operation, you will need only seven people to operate it. You expect the new equipment to be installed in about six months.

You will find other jobs in your company for the eight people who will not be needed.

2. The Case of the New Method

You are supervisor of a department that assembles small radios.

There are six stations in the assembly line; the worker at each station performs one part of the assembly and passes the radio to the next station.

You have decided that the use of job enrichment will improve the challenge of each job and will create more satisfaction on the part of the employees. Also, you feel that it will result in higher productivity.

Therefore, you are going to have each worker assemble the entire radio instead of doing only one part. Each radio will have a number attached to it to identify the worker who assembled it.

3. The Case of the New Policy

You are the foreman of a machine shop.

In recent months, your workers have been taking various amounts of time to wash up and get ready to go home at the end of the shift. Some have taken as much as 30 minutes. Others have taken as little as five. You have had no specific rules covering the amount of time they should take. You have not told anyone that he or she was taking too long.

To increase productivity, top management and you have agreed to implement a new policy that workers will be allowed a maximum of 10 minutes to wash up before their shift ends.

4. The Case of the Loss-Producing Product

You are supervisor of a group in an assembly department.

You received the order for a new product that was based on assembling 130 units per day. This figure had been arrived at to get the bid. Also, your engineers and top manufacturing management had agreed that it could be done. You were not consulted on the number your people could assemble.

You have a long-term contract and you are losing money every day. You cannot change the price to the customer, and you must increase productivity to stay in business.

This approach to case studies is one that can be readily adapted to a particular situation in your organization. Cases can be written to describe a typical situation. Each group should be given 30-45 minutes to analyze a case. The chairperson or secretary of the group will report to the entire group on its case. The case study would then be open to discussion by the entire group. The leader has the key role of supplementing and commenting on the principles, approaches, and techniques that have come from the discussion to tie the case study into the objectives of that particular session.

Following is a more complicated case study that could be used or modified for a training meeting. For this meeting, assume you have just been appointed division manager in Bell Tone Corporation's largest region. Bell Tone is a leading manufacturer and distributor of bells. They manufacture and sell every conceivable type of bell, both electrical and manual.

Reporting to you are district engineering managers, district sales managers, district service managers, plus an administrative and clerical staff—15 people total.

You and your regional manager have discussed some broad goals that you have mutually agreed should become part of your division's common goals.

These were in the area of service improvement, revenue improvement, and development of people. Although you didn't like to agree to these broad objectives prior to talking with your division team, this is the condition under which the job was offered and you accepted it.

Roles You Must Fulfill in Conducting the Meeting

Assume that in planning the meeting, you feel that your objectives are to inform the participants of the broad division objectives to which you had agreed and get their acceptance of them. Your approach will be to present information, encourage and control discussion, and get the group to agree with the objectives. In doing this, you will need to play the role of presenter, facilitator, and decision maker. You may want to end the meeting by telling the participants that you will meet with them individually to reach agreement on their roles in setting and accomplishing the objectives that apply to their department.

Role Playing

Role playing is a training technique in which one or more members of the training group takes a role that is assigned. For example, in "The Case of the New Policy," one of the group members will be asked to play the part of a foreman. The conference leader can take the part of an employee who feels that 10 minutes is not enough time to wash up before the shift ends. In front of the group, the foreman will then conduct a discussion with the employee. The rest of the group will observe the role playing and will comment on it after it is finished.

Another possible approach to role playing is called "multiple role playing." This means that all members of the training class will participate at the same time. Half of them will take the role of supervisor and the other half will take the role of employee. They will all be buzzing at the same time. After a period of this multiple role playing, open discussions will analyze the situation from the standpoint of both the supervisor and the employee. If the multiple role playing is repeated, each individual will take the opposite role. A modification of this is to have three roles: supervisor, employee, and observer. Instead of having the supervisor and the employee describe their experience, the observer can describe it along with any comments and suggestions from the supervisor and employee.

Role playing can be very effective in supervisory training. It involves the group and maintains high interest and enjoyment on the part of participants. Furthermore, it can be very helpful in the learning process. By participating in a role-playing situation, people will learn better than by just listening to somebody discuss it. By observing a role-playing situation, supervisors can see things happen and discuss it as a case study.

Tests

Tests can be used for several purposes in an instructional meeting. They must be related to the subject content and objectives of the meeting or series of meetings. Before a training program starts, a pretest can be administered to measure the level of knowledge and attitudes of participants before any instruction has been given. This will help to determine the specific needs to be met in the meeting. For example, if everyone answers certain questions correctly, the topic can be eliminated from the course material. If, on the other hand, the test responses show a complete lack of knowledge on a particular topic, considerable time and effort should be spent during the instructional meeting to be sure the students learn it.

At the end of a training program, a posttest can be administered to measure levels of knowledge and attitudes. The responses to the posttest can be compared to the pretest responses to evaluate the program in terms of the learning that has taken place. (See chapter 12 on evaluation.)

In addition to determining needs and evaluating the program, tests can be effectively used as discussion tools. When participants spend their time and energy to take a test, they are most anxious to see how they did. They are also eager to explain the reasons for their answers and sometimes dogmatically defend them. This can lead to enthusiastic and sometimes heated discussions. Under the guidance and control of an effective leader, the discussion can help to accomplish the objectives of the meeting in a manner that is both enjoyable and beneficial to the participants.

The tests can be written by the coordinator or the instructor of the training meeting. Or, a standardized test can be purchased for use in the course. The first approach offers the advantage of being tailored to the organization and the subject content being planned. It requires considerable time and test construction know-how to be effective.

The standardized test can be reasonably purchased as an off-the-shelf item. A manual usually accompanies the test to provide information on the uses and administration of the test. It also includes norms that have been gathered from other organizations.

An example of a standardized test is the Supervisory Inventory on Communication (SIC) that can be given to participants in the beginning of a training program on communications. The SIC can be scored by the participants. The test can then be used effectively as a device for stimulating lively and beneficial discussion. The conference leader would encourage individuals to state answers and reasons for them. Other participants can disagree and give their reasons. The leader can then give the scoring key answer and rationale provided by the author. The leader can add personal comments and draw conclusions pertinent to the group. The manual of the SIC includes suggestions for using the test as well as the rationale for each answer.

Any test can be used in the same way to make training meetings interesting as well as beneficial. Some suggestions for using standardized tests follow:

- Be sure the test content is related to the subject content and objectives of the session.
- Administer the test at the start of the program.
- Score the test and return it to participants (or allow participants to score their own).
- Select items for discussion that will be of greatest interest and benefit to the group.
- Encourage participants to argue both sides of the question during the discussion.
- Provide the participants with the rationale for the correct answer that was developed by the author.
- Summarize the discussion and the principle or technique that was illustrated by the test item.

Games and Exercises

Another approach in training meetings is to use games and exercises. Typically, in this technique, the trainees are divided into small groups and given a realistic situation to address. They compete with each other and are judged on some basics of effectiveness, usually in terms of productivity, profits, sales, or similar criteria. Management games can be purchased from a number of sources or can be created for the particular session. Some games are very simple and require less than an hour of meeting time. Others are complicated and use the computer.

The four steps in table 10-1 provide a short summary for any meeting. Details are found in other chapters.

Table 10-1. The Four-Step Approach for Conducting a Meeting.

1. Opening the meeting	Get the attention of the participants and clarify the objectives of the meeting.
2. Imparting information	Present other pertinent information.
3. Facilitating discussion	Serve as a catalyst in stimulating and controlling discussion.
4. Concluding the meeting	Get the group to agree with the objectives and their roles in accomplishing them. End on a positive note, and thank them for their participation. If you are planning to get together with each person, clarify what you want to accomplish and how you will make contact. Also, tell them if and when the next meeting will be held.

Chapter 11

How to Conduct a Problem-Solving Meeting

A problem-solving meeting is probably the most difficult to conduct. It requires the leader to integrate several types of meetings into one. Included in a problem-solving meeting are information giving, information getting, and possibly brainstorming. It requires the leader to play several roles: presenter, listener, catalyst, arbitrator, facilitator, and participant. And it usually includes many of the situations that can make a meeting difficult to control. In short, the leader has a big challenge to make the meeting productive.

> **Do—**
> Open with a bang, not a sour note that spells defeat or discouragement.

Preparation

The preparation for a problem-solving meeting includes some planning that is unique to this type of meeting. For example, in conducting an information-giving or instructional meeting, much of the planning involves the gathering of information and preparing to present it. In a problem-solving meeting, much of the preparation time is spent deciding on questions to ask. The question becomes the chief tool of the problem-solving leader. Also, the proper sequence of questions must be carefully planned.

Steps in a Problem-Solving Meeting

STEP 1. CLEAR STATEMENT OF THE PROBLEM

Someone once said, "A problem well defined is a problem half solved." Perhaps it is a slight exaggeration, but it has truth in it. A productive, problem-solving conference must start with a clear statement of the problem.

Planning for a Problem-Solving Conference

The following steps in a problem-solving conference indicate the kind of preparation that is needed.

I. Introduction (a two- to three-minute talk to get attention)
- story related to the subject
- explanation of why the group is there
- explanation of how the group can help solve the problem
- dramatic examples of the problem
- clear statement of the problem.

II. Solving the Problem

Questions beginning with who, what, when, why, where, and how are usually most effective.

Some suggestions are
- causes
  - What caused the problem?
  - Why do we have the problem?
- suggested solutions
  - What can be done to improve the situation?
  - What suggestions do you have for solving the problem?
  - How can we . . . ?
- best solutions
  - Of the ideas you've suggested, which ones seem to be the best ones?
  - Which of these suggestions don't seem to be practical?
  - What is the best solution to our problem?

III. Summary and Conclusions
- What is the problem?
- What has been decided?
- What will be done about it?

Here are some examples of practical problems that are clearly and succinctly stated:

Absenteeism

How can we reduce absenteeism by 25 percent by December 31?

Turnover

How can we reduce turnover among hourly employees to 3 percent by March 31?

Quality

How can we reduce the scrap rate from 5 percent to 4 percent by July 31?

Paperwork

How can we reduce the amount of paperwork that is required of our production people?

Sales

How can we get 10 percent of the market by the end of this fiscal period?

Finance

How can we double our return-on-investment during the next fiscal year?

Training

How, in minimum time, can we do an effective job of training new employees so they will be safe, productive, and happy?

Meetings

How can we reduce the amount of time that is wasted in our production meetings?

Morale

How can we improve the attitudes of our engineers?

Motivation

How can we get our clerical employees to be enthusiastic toward their jobs?

Communications

How can we improve our downward communications to first-line production supervisors?

All of these problems begin with "How can we . . . ." These statements immediately tell the participants that they are going to help solve the problem. The statements also clearly indicate the kind of problem they must help solve.

The first step in problem solving requires the leader to select the problem and clearly define it.

STEP 2. REASONS WHY THE PROBLEM MUST BE SOLVED

This section of the meeting must convince the participants that the meeting is necessary. It should also persuade them that this is the place they should be. It should build enthusiasm for the meeting because solving the problem will be of benefit to them and the organization.

It should also present facts and other information to sell the group on the need for solving the problem.

STEP 3. CAUSES OF THE PROBLEM

In preparing for this phase of the problem-solving conference, the leader should plan to get causes (facts and opinions) from the group. In addition, the leader should gather information so that he or she can also present any causes not identified by the group. The specific question "What are the causes of the problem?" is the key question that should be present for this phase of the meeting.

STEP 4. POSSIBLE SOLUTIONS

Again, the preparation of the leader centers on the particular question to ask. In addition, the leader should think of possible solutions in case they aren't suggested by participants.

This phase is probably the most interesting and enjoyable phase of a problem-solving meeting. Here is where the brainstorming technique should be used. The leader should introduce this part of the meeting with such words as:

"We have just analyzed the causes of the problem as we see them. Now we are going to consider possible solutions. We aren't going to do it the way we usually do when we face a problem. What we usually do is have someone suggest a solution and the rest of us evaluate it and agree or disagree. If we don't agree on that one, someone else suggests a solution and we follow the same process of evaluation. As we know, all of us are human. And if anyone shoots down our idea, our feelings become hurt and we tend to pout, react negatively to the idea of the one who criticized our solution, and show other similar behavior. When we use this process, hard feelings frequently develop and many possible solutions are never suggested, both because of a shortage of time and because we hold them back for a fear they'll be shot down.

"Today, we are going to use brainstorming and concentrate all of our knowledge, creativity, and energy to list all of the possible solutions we can think of. Our next step will be to evaluate each idea, compare it with others, and agree on the best one or more that will solve the problem. We won't even remember who suggested what idea.

"Now, here are the rules for brainstorming: (Put them on a flipchart.)

- Quantity, not quality, counts. Let's get down a lot of possible solutions. This way we'll be sure that we don't miss any. And a certain percentage of them are bound to be good.

- Freewheeling is encouraged. Don't worry whether the idea is practical or ridiculous. Don't worry how much time it will take or how much it will cost. Don't even think about whether we've tried it before. And don't consider whether it fits into our company philosophy or policy. All of these considerations will be applied in the next phase of our meeting.

- Piggybacking or hitchhiking is encouraged. Listen to the ideas of others; they may trigger an idea in your mind.

- No evaluation or judgment is allowed. When someone presents a solution, don't try to evaluate it. Just concentrate on solutions you can suggest.

"Our slogan is 'Think up or Shut up.'"

In preparing for this phase, the leader should prepare a question such as "What are all the possible solutions?" The leader must be on the alert for judgment and evaluation because this is the way most people have been taught to think and act.

STEP 5. THE BEST SOLUTION

As promised in Step 4, this is the time to compare and evaluate. Some criteria will be necessary to use when comparing the possible solutions that have been developed. For example, each possible solution may be judged according to the following:

- Will it solve the problem? Some of the solutions may not fit.
- Is it within the budget? Some solutions may be too costly.
- How long will it take? Try to establish a timeframe so certain solutions will be eliminated because they will take too long.
- Is it within company policy? This may not be an absolute criterion because the policy might be bent or changed if the solution is good enough.
- Can it be implemented effectively? If the people who have to implement the solution won't accept it, it might be necessary to modify or eliminate it.

The agreed-on criteria should be applied to sort the possible solutions into the following categories:

- looks good (+)
- possible (?)
- eliminate (−).

This can be done quite readily. The next step is to analyze the possible ones more carefully. With further discussion and possible modification, they should be sorted into one of the other two categories and should be followed by a + or −.

The next step (and the most difficult one) is to agree on the best solution. Frequently, the best solution is a combination of several possible solutions. It also may have several parts to it and even a Plan A (let's try this first) and Plan B (let's try this if Plan A doesn't work).

STEP 6. IMPLEMENTATION OF THE SOLUTION

It is very important to include this final phase in a problem-solving meeting. Many good solutions have failed because little thought and no plans were devoted to the implementation of the solution. The leader can ask the group, "How should we implement the decision?" The question can trigger another problem-solving meeting. Brainstorming may again be in order to be followed by judicial thinking and agreement on the best way to implement the decision.

> **Do—**
> Leave the participants with an immediate action program and realistic objectives.

When the implementation approach is agreed on, the leader might give out assignments to one or more members of the group. The important factor is that implementation is discussed and agreed on in the meeting so that the solution will be effective.

Participation

To have a productive problem-solving meeting where the participants are learning and retaining information, participation is essential. Here are some guidelines.

Getting Participation

Obviously, a problem-solving meeting will not be effective unless the participants take part. Here are some ways to ensure active participation:

- Select the right people. Criteria should include those who can contribute to solving the problem as well as those who are important to implementing the solution. The number of participants should probably be in the six to eight range.
- Select the right time. Be sure the participants can conveniently attend and devote their complete attention to the problem.
- Have proper physical facilities. Make it conducive to participation (for example, gather around a table). Have everything ready.
- Be sure your questions are clear. Put them on the whiteboard or flipchart.
- Make the participants feel important. Ask for their ideas; listen to their comments; be receptive to their ideas, even if they're different from your own; give them credit for their contributions.
- Maintain a climate that fosters participation. Don't embarrass or ridicule any of the participants. And, as the leader, don't dominate.

Controlling Participation

In a problem-solving meeting, it is usually easy for the leader to get participation. The difficult part may be in controlling the participation. As described in chapter 9, the most effective way to control a meeting is to keep it from getting out of control. The best way to do this is to carefully prepare each phase of the meeting, including the exact questions that will be asked. Even if this is done, the meeting may get out of control at times. For example, two or more of the people may get into a heated argument over what the best solution is or how it should be implemented.

The most common problem is that participants get so involved that they get ahead of the leader. They frequently suggest solutions when the leader is discussing causes. And this often happens even if the leader has cautioned against it. This isn't a serious control problem, however, because it is easy for the leader to bring it back on the track without embarrassing the person. The leader can simply say (perhaps with a little humor):

> "Joe, you've just given us a possible solution because you are so anxious to get this problem solved. Right now we are still on causes of the problem. Please hold that comment until we get to the next phase of our meeting."

This control problem might have been prevented and certainly very easily solved if the leader had put all the steps of the meeting on the chalkboard or flipchart at the beginning of the meeting and left them there during the entire meeting. This would be a constant reminder so that participants would know exactly where they are and where they are going.

A problem-solving meeting should use the six-step approach:

1. clear statement of the problem
2. why the problem must be solved
3. causes of the problem
4. possible solutions
5. the best solution
6. implementation of the solution.

Managers can reach quality decisions and get high acceptance by using these steps.

Chapter 12

How to Evaluate and Improve a Meeting

Evaluating Meetings

To improve future meetings, leaders need some evaluation of the effectiveness of the meetings they conduct. There are three possible sources for the evaluation of a meeting:

1. self-evaluation by the leader
2. evaluation by a trained observer
3. evaluation by participants.

All of these sources can be helpful. The worth of the evaluation will depend on the objectivity of the evaluator as well as the effectiveness of the forms and procedures that are used. Let's consider each approach separately.

Self-Evaluation by the Leader

After the meeting is over, the leader can ask, "How did I do?" To answer the question, the leader needs guidelines or standards to use. Also, the leader must be careful to be objective and look at the meeting as an outsider would.

Table 12-1 was developed to be used in a leader's self-evaluation of a meeting. It considers the satisfaction of the participants as well as the accomplishment of objectives in minimum time.

The completion of table 12-1 will take concentration and objectivity. If it is completed and analyzed as soon as every meeting is over, great improvements could be made in future meetings by the leader.

Table 12-1. Self-Evaluation of a Meeting.

A. Objectives

1. What were the meeting objectives?
2. Were they accomplished?
   ☐ Yes   ☐ No   ☐ Partially
3. Which objectives were not completely accomplished?
   Why not? (Be specific.) _____

   _____

   _____

B. Time

1. Were objectives accomplished in minimum time?
   ☐ Yes   ☐ No   ☐ Not Sure
2. If objectives were not accomplished in minimum time, why not? (Be specific.)_____

   _____

   _____

C. Participants

In your opinion, how satisfied were participants with the meeting?
   ☐ Very Satisfied   ☐ Satisfied   ☐ Dissatisfied   ☐ Very Dissatisfied

D. If I were conducting the meeting again, what would I do the same? What would I do differently?

	Same	Different	Comments
1. Location			
2. Scheduled Time			
3. Selection of Participants			
4. Objectives			
5. Room Setup			
6. Audiovisual Aids			
7. Agenda			
8. My Own Preparation			

D. If I were conducting the meeting again, what would I do the same? What would I do differently (continued)?	Same	Different	Comments
9. Advance Notice to Participants			
10. Introduction			
11. Amount of Presentation by Me			
12. Amount of Participation from Group			
13. Conclusion			
What else would I do differently?			

Evaluation by a Trained Observer

A trained observer is one who knows the ingredients of a productive meeting. This person would sit in the back of the room and objectively observe during the meeting. A form would be helpful to guide the evaluation.

If the person is making a presentation, a relatively simple form (table 12-2) can be completed by the observer and discussed with the speaker.

A more sophisticated approach is needed if the meeting consists of more than a simple presentation. Tables 12-3 and 12-4 were developed for completion during and after the meeting. In addition, the observer should have a pad of paper to record comments and suggestions as the meeting progresses. The notes can be coded to the form (for example, A3 on table 12-3 would be a comment concerning noise).

Table 12-4, to be completed by the trained observer after the program, is identical to sections A, B, and C of table 12-1 to be completed by the leader. If both people complete these forms independently, it will provide an excellent opportunity to compare notes and reach agreement on what can be done to improve future meetings.

Some leaders may not appreciate frank and critical comments from a trained observer. Therefore, a word of advice is needed for both the leader and the trained observer:

- *Advice for meeting leader:* Be receptive to the comments of the trained observer. Don't be defensive. Recognize that the trained observer has one purpose: to help you improve future meetings.

Table 12-2. Evaluation by a Trained Observer.

	Poor	Fair	Good	Very Good	Excellent
1. Statement of Objectives Comment:	☐	☐	☐	☐	☐
2. Presentation Effectiveness Comment:	☐	☐	☐	☐	☐
3. Ratio of Presentation to Participation Comment:	☐	☐	☐	☐	☐
4. Control of the Meeting Comment:	☐	☐	☐	☐	☐
5. Use of Aids Comment:	☐	☐	☐	☐	☐
6. Effectiveness of Group Involvement Comment:	☐	☐	☐	☐	☐
7. Conclusion of Meeting Comment:	☐	☐	☐	☐	☐
8. Overall Effectiveness Comment:	☐	☐	☐	☐	☐

Suggestions for Improvement:

Table 12-3. Detailed Evaluation of Meeting Productivity by a Trained Observer.

(To be completed during the meeting)

	Poor	Fair	Good	Very Good	Excellent
A. Physical Facilities					
1. Room setup	☐	☐	☐	☐	☐
2. Temperature	☐	☐	☐	☐	☐
3. Quiet	☐	☐	☐	☐	☐
4. Comfortable	☐	☐	☐	☐	☐
5. Ventilation	☐	☐	☐	☐	☐
B. Introduction					
1. Start on time	☐	☐	☐	☐	☐
2. Create interest and attention	☐	☐	☐	☐	☐
3. Clarify objectives	☐	☐	☐	☐	☐
C. Main Body					
1. Information clearly presented	☐	☐	☐	☐	☐
2. Ratio of presentation to discussion	☐	☐	☐	☐	☐
D. Audiovisual Aids					
1. Selection	☐	☐	☐	☐	☐
2. Use	☐	☐	☐	☐	☐
E. Attitude of Leader Toward Group	☐	☐	☐	☐	☐
F. Maintenance of Interest and Enthusiasm	☐	☐	☐	☐	☐
G. Handling of People Problems (off subject, talk too much, etc.)	☐	☐	☐	☐	☐
H. Control of Meeting	☐	☐	☐	☐	☐
I. Conclusion					
1. Summary of meeting	☐	☐	☐	☐	☐
2. Accomplishment of objectives	☐	☐	☐	☐	☐
3. Final comments (thank participants, assignments, next meeting, etc.)	☐	☐	☐	☐	☐
4. End meeting on time	☐	☐	☐	☐	☐

Table 12-4. Evaluation of Meeting Productivity by a Trained Observer.

(To be completed immediately after the meeting)

A. Objectives

  1. What were the meeting objectives?

    _____

    _____

  2. Were they accomplished?

    ☐ Yes   ☐ No   ☐ Partially

  3. Which objectives were not completely accomplished?

    Why not? (Be specific.)_____

    _____

    _____

B. Time

  1. Were objectives accomplished in minimum time?

    ☐ Yes   ☐ No   ☐ Not Sure

  2. If objectives were not accomplished in minimum time, why not? (Be specific.) _____

    _____

    _____

C. Participants

In your opinion, how satisfied were participants with the meeting?

  ☐ Very Satisfied   ☐ Satisfied   ☐ Dissatisfied   ☐ Very Dissatisfied

---

- *Advice for trained observer:* Be tactful as well as objective. Compliment as well as criticize. Remember, most people don't like to be criticized, even if you are trying to help. Think of yourself as a salesperson with ideas to help your customer (the leader). If he or she doesn't buy what you have to say, your time has been wasted and perhaps your relationship has worsened.

    Your objective is to help, not criticize, so act accordingly.

Do—
Recognize good performance.

Evaluation by Participants

Participants provide a good source for evaluation. Like the leader, they may not be able to be as objective as a trained observer. But they can provide valuable feedback to help the leader improve meeting effectiveness. The type of meeting would determine the specific forms to use. But there are five guidelines to get honest and meaningful reactions to all types of meetings:

1. Determine what kind of information you want (subject, leader, facilities, schedule, handouts, visual aids, etc.).
2. Prepare a written form to get reaction from participants.
3. Design the form so the information can be tabulated and quantified. Do not use open questions like, "How well did you like the program?" or "What did you like best?" These questions take much longer to answer and are less meaningful.
4. Allow participants to add comments that will help explain their reactions and offer suggestions for improvement. A good question is, "What would have made the meeting more effective?" or "How could the meeting have been improved?"
5. Obtain honest reactions by removing any fear of repercussions for negative comments. The best way to do this is to make the forms anonymous and have participants put them on a table on their way out of the meeting.

As examples, let's consider an instructional meeting and then a staff meeting to illustrate the kinds of forms and procedures that should be followed to get honest and helpful reactions.

EXAMPLE: EVALUATING AN INSTRUCTIONAL MEETING

Why Ask for Participant Reactions?

The purpose of instructional meetings is to help the participants improve their behavior and the results they accomplish. If instructors are trying to help them, their reactions will tell to what extent they are helped as they see it. This feedback to the leader is very important for several reasons:

- The process of asking for their reactions tells the participants that the instructor is learner-oriented. And the leader should consider them customers and recognize the importance of getting positive reactions.
- The reactions indicate the level of satisfaction of the participants—one of the three ingredients of a productive meeting. These are the reactions the trainees will carry back to the job. These feelings can affect their entire attitude— toward the job, toward the organization, and toward the training itself. If the reactions are negative, the entire training program can receive a black eye and even be eliminated if the news gets to high-level executives.
- The reactions could be closely related to the learning that takes place. Positive reactions indicate a high level of interest and a good climate for

learning to take place. Negative reactions indicate such things as lack of interest, disappointment, desire to be elsewhere, and lack of respect for the conference leader or speaker. These attitudes are not conducive toward learning.

- Specific comments can suggest areas of meeting improvement that the leader or the trained observer did not see. These can be very helpful in improving future meetings.

When Should You Ask for Participant Reaction?

It is important to get reactions from all participants immediately after the program is over. Ask the participants to complete their forms and turn them in before leaving the room. This way the leader can get 100 percent response without being able to identify the reactions from any person. If a leader allows the reaction to be delayed, the leader is almost sure to get less than 100 percent response and sometimes as low as 20 percent.

Delayed response may rate the meeting as being better, worse, or the same as an immediate response. If the leader wants delayed response also, that's fine. But be sure to get immediate response and feedback because that is what they will take back to their jobs. A comparison of immediate with delayed responses may be helpful in evaluating the meeting and deciding on improvements.

How to Obtain Honest Participants' Reactions

A form should be designed and used to incorporate the five important guidelines described previously:

1. Determine the information you want.
2. Use a written form.
3. Design the form so it can be tabulated and quantified.
4. Encourage written comments and suggestions.
5. Obtain honest reactions by making it anonymous.

At the Management Institute, University of Wisconsin in Milwaukee, two forms are used. Table 12-5 is used to evaluate each leader who conducts an instructional meeting. It obtains reactions to the subject, leader, facilities, and meals. It is designed so the forms can be tabulated and quantified. It does not require or even suggest a signature. It encourages comments and suggestions for improvement. It is completed by each participant and put in a pile as the participant leaves the room. It does obtain honest and meaningful reactions from the participants concerning their satisfaction with the entire meeting and various phases of it.

Table 12-5. Reaction Sheet.

Please give your frank reactions and comments. They will help evaluate this program for possible improvement.

Leader_____ Subject_____ Date_____

1. How do you rate the subject content?
    ☐ Excellent   ☐ Very Good   ☐ Good   ☐ Fair   ☐ Poor
    Comments:

2. How do you rate the leader?
    ☐ Excellent   ☐ Very Good   ☐ Good   ☐ Fair   ☐ Poor
    Comments:

3. What benefits do you feel you got from this session?
    ☐ New knowledge that is pertinent
    ☐ Specific approaches, skills, or techniques that I can apply on the job
    ☐ Change of attitude that will help me in my job
    ☐ Other: _____

4. What is your overall rating of the meeting?
    ☐ Excellent   ☐ Very Good   ☐ Good   ☐ Fair   ☐ Poor
    Comments:

5. How were the meeting facilities?
    ☐ Excellent   ☐ Very Good   ☐ Good   ☐ Fair   ☐ Poor
    Comments:

6. How was the meal? (If appropriate)
    ☐ Excellent   ☐ Very Good   ☐ Good   ☐ Fair   ☐ Poor
    Comments:

7. What would have made this session better?

Where several leaders appear on the same program, a final comment sheet is also used as shown in table 12-6. This provides an overall reaction, which can be quantified and analyzed for improving future programs. The example of the evaluation of an instructional meeting (table 12-5) illustrates a number of principles for obtaining participants' reactions to a meeting. First of all, it tells the participants that the leader wants to conduct productive meetings and wants their help in doing it. This process can have a positive effect on the participants.

Also, it provides the leader with accurate information on the level of satisfaction of the participants, which is one of the three ingredients of a productive meeting. The leader and the trained observer can never be quite sure of the level of satisfaction of participants, particularly if the leader is a manager of the participants. The participants can leave the meeting with apparent enthusiasm and satisfaction, but their mood changes when they get out the sight of the leader. They may even tell the leader that it was a fine meeting because they want to impress him or her, but they might tell their peers that it was a waste of time.

The benefits of participant reaction to the leader can be great if five conditions exist:

1. The leader really wants to improve future meetings.
2. The leader sincerely wants honest reactions from participants.
3. The participants aren't afraid to give honest reactions and suggestions.
4. The leader reacts positively to the feedback, whether positive or negative.
5. The leader incorporates some of the comments and suggestions into future meetings.

EXAMPLE: EVALUATING A STAFF MEETING

If the leader is evaluating a staff or departmental meeting, table 12-7 can be used or adapted to the situation.

It is obvious that the completion of table 12-7 is going to take quite a bit of time. It is important to allow the 15 to 20 minutes that will be required. It's also pretty obvious that this form should not be used at the end of every staff or departmental meeting. The best approach would be to explain it and distribute it at the end of a particular staff meeting. The reactions should then be tabulated and summarized. The leader should study them and incorporate whatever suggestions will help improve future staff meetings. At a later time (perhaps six to 10 staff meetings later), the same procedure and form can be used to see whether improvements have been made as the participants see it. Participants who complete a form like table 12-7 will be watching closely to see if the meeting leader makes any changes.

Improving Future Meetings

Three separate but related approaches have been suggested for evaluating meetings. The first calls for a self-evaluation by the meeting leader immediately after the meeting. The second uses a trained observer who evaluates the meeting while in progress and supplements it with an evaluation immediately after the meeting

Table 12-6. Final Comment Sheet for Participants.

Name of Program_____ Date_____

1. How would you rate the overall program as an educational experience?
   ☐ Excellent ☐ Very Good ☐ Good ☐ Fair ☐ Poor
   Comments:

2. To what extent will the program help you do a better job for your organization?
   ☐ To a large extent ☐ To some extent ☐ Very little
   Comments:

3. What were the major benefits you received? (Check all that apply.)
   ☐ Helped confirm some of my ideas
   ☐ Presented new ideas and approaches
   ☐ Acquainted me with problems and solutions from others
   ☐ Gave me a good chance to look objectively at myself and my job
   Comments:

4. How were the meeting facilities?
   ☐ Excellent ☐ Very Good ☐ Good ☐ Fair ☐ Poor
   Comments:

5. How would you rate the meal? (If appropriate)
   ☐ Excellent ☐ Very Good ☐ Good ☐ Fair ☐ Poor
   Comments:

6. Would you like to attend future programs of a similar nature?
   ☐ Yes ☐ No ☐ Not Sure
   Comments:

7. What do you suggest for improving future meetings?

Name (optional)_____

ends. The third approach elicits reactions from the participants. Examples have been given for both an instructional and staff meeting.

Which approach is best? The more the better. Each of the three can provide helpful information. The use of two of the three procedures will provide information from two sources to reinforce or challenge the evaluation of each. The use of all three will provide the most helpful data.

Table 12-7. Evaluation of a Departmental Meeting.

(To be completed by participants at the end of the meeting)

1. Was the meeting held at the best possible time?
    ☐ Yes   ☐ No   ☐ Uncertain
    Comments:

2. Was the meeting held at the best possible place?
    ☐ Yes   ☐ No   ☐ Uncertain
    Comments:

3. Were the objectives of the meeting clear to you?
    ☐ Yes   ☐ No   ☐ Uncertain
    Comments:

4. Were the objectives accomplished?
    ☐ Yes   ☐ No   ☐ Uncertain
    Comments:

5. How was the length of the meeting?
    ☐ OK   ☐ Too long   ☐ Too short
    Comments:

6. How well prepared was the leader?
    ☐ Very well   ☐ Pretty well   ☐ Not prepared
    Comments:

7. Did the instructor get and hold your interest?
    ☐ Yes   ☐ No
    Comments:

8. How well did the leader get and maintain your enthusiasm?
    ☐ Very well   ☐ Pretty well   ☐ Poorly
    Comments:

9. How well did you understand what was going on during the entire meeting?
    ☐ Very well   ☐ Pretty well   ☐ Poorly
    Comments:

---

10. How was the conclusion of the meeting?

    ☐ Excellent   ☐ Very Good   ☐ Good   ☐ Fair   ☐ Poor

    Comments:

11. How satisfied are you as a participant of the meeting?

    ☐ Very satisfied   ☐ Satisfied   ☐ Neutral   ☐ Dissatisfied   ☐ Very dissatisfied

    Comments:

12. How would you rate the meeting in terms of accomplishing objectives in minimum time with satisfied participants?

    ☐ Excellent   ☐ Very Good   ☐ Good   ☐ Fair   ☐ Poor

    Comments:

As a starter, each meeting leader should at least use the self-evaluation approach. If a trained observer is available, this should be done on a selected basis. The meeting leader should be sure that the trained observer doesn't interfere with the effectiveness of the meeting just by being there. The leader may want to introduce the trained observer and explain the purpose.

Regarding the evaluation by participants, reaction sheets should be used immediately in all instructional meetings. Tables 12-5 and 12-6 can be used or adapted to get honest and meaningful reactions. These reactions and comments should be carefully analyzed by the meeting instructors and coordinators, and meeting changes should be made accordingly.

Regarding the evaluation of staff or departmental meetings by the participants, proceed with caution. A leader shouldn't do it if he or she doesn't want honest reactions and if the leader doesn't plan to incorporate changes. A leader must be willing to swallow some pride and accept critical reactions from subordinates. Some leaders may not be able to do this. They will probably go on conducting their meetings the same way, whether productive or nonproductive. But those leaders who are willing to accept criticism and suggestions from subordinates in their staff meetings can be richly rewarded with more productive meetings to the benefit of all.

Regarding meetings, practice improves performance under two conditions:

1. You practice the right things.
2. You are being critiqued, coached, and helped to improve.

Obviously, the first condition requires a person to know the ingredients of a productive meeting. The second condition requires critical analysis of meetings to suggest ways to improve. This section of the book has described three ways to evaluate, analyze the information, and look for ways to improve. You must provide the desire. As the old saying goes, "You can lead a horse to water, but you can't make it drink!"

Do—
Stress importance of communication.

Posttest

➤

What Do You Know About Productive Meetings?

Review each statement about meetings, and mark whether you agree or disagree.

Agree	Disagree		
☐	☐	1.	A meeting is the best way to communicate information to a group of people.
☐	☐	2.	A meeting is the best way to get information from several people.
☐	☐	3.	A meeting is necessary when there is a problem to solve.
☐	☐	4.	A meeting is the best way to train and develop people.
☐	☐	5.	A meeting is productive if the leader's objectives are accomplished.
☐	☐	6.	A meeting is productive if the leader's objectives are accomplished in a minimum amount of time.
☐	☐	7.	A meeting is productive if the leader's objectives are accomplished in a minimum amount of time with satisfied participants.
☐	☐	8.	The cost of a meeting can usually be accurately determined.
☐	☐	9.	The benefits of a meeting can usually be accurately determined.
☐	☐	10.	One of the most costly aspects of nonproductive meetings can be the negative attitudes on the part of those attending.
☐	☐	11.	Most of the causes of nonproductive meetings are under the control of the leader.
☐	☐	12.	Bad scheduling can result in nonproductive meetings.
☐	☐	13.	Poor facilities can contribute to nonproductive meetings.

Agree	Disagree	
☐	☐	14. A meeting leader is more effective as a catalyst than a strong leader.
☐	☐	15. To have a productive meeting, all or nearly all of the participants must take an active part.
☐	☐	16. Time scheduling is important to a meeting's success.
☐	☐	17. Physical facilities are important to the success of the meeting.
☐	☐	18. An important part of preparation is to be sure that the right people are attending.
☐	☐	19. A flipchart, overhead projector, Microsoft PowerPoint, or other audiovisual aid should be standard equipment for every meeting.
☐	☐	20. If the leader has properly planned for physical facilities and audiovisual aids, there is no reason to check on them prior to the meeting.
☐	☐	21. Proper advance notice to participants is important for productive meetings.
☐	☐	22. Microsoft PowerPoint is more effective than using aids such as the flipchart and overhead projector.
☐	☐	23. The shorter a presentation, the more effective it is.
☐	☐	24. Humor always improves the effectiveness of a presentation.
☐	☐	25. The Kirkpatrick PIE (practical, interactive, and enjoyable) approach should be used by all meeting leaders.
☐	☐	26. If a participant asks a question, it should be answered in the meeting.
☐	☐	27. Overhead questions should be used more frequently than direct questions.
☐	☐	28. A question-and-answer period is a good way to end a meeting.
☐	☐	29. The amount of enthusiasm by participants is directly related to their participation.
☐	☐	30. Fear of being embarrassed or ridiculed by the leader is a frequent cause of nonparticipation and lack of enthusiasm.
☐	☐	31. Enthusiasm on the part of the leader begets enthusiasm.
☐	☐	32. Participants should leave the meeting thinking, "I'm glad I came!"

Agree	Disagree	
☐	☐	33. A leader should start the meeting on time even if some of the participants aren't there.
☐	☐	34. The introductory part of a meeting should get the attention of the participants and clarify meeting objectives.
☐	☐	35. It is easier to get participation than to control a meeting.
☐	☐	36. The best way to control a meeting is to prevent it from getting out of control.
☐	☐	37. If a participant is causing problems, the leader should handle the situation without embarrassing or ridiculing the participant.
☐	☐	38. A leader should always maintain self-control in a meeting.
☐	☐	39. When introducing a speaker, the chairperson should remember that the shorter the introduction the better.
☐	☐	40. When making a presentation, the presenter is more effective when using Microsoft PowerPoint than overhead transparencies.
☐	☐	41. It's the responsibility of the chairperson, not the speaker, to be sure the meeting runs on schedule.
☐	☐	42. A leader can always tell whether the meeting has been productive.
☐	☐	43. Participants can always tell whether the meeting has been productive.
☐	☐	44. A trained observer can always tell whether the meeting has been productive.
☐	☐	45. An instructor should use the leader, participants, and trained observer to determine whether the meeting has been productive.
☐	☐	46. The objective of instructor-led meetings is to increase knowledge, increase skills, or change attitudes.
☐	☐	47. The most important factor in instructor-led meetings is the effectiveness of the leader.
☐	☐	48. Trainers from within the organization are more effective than outside consultants.
☐	☐	49. In instructor-led meetings, the more participation the better.
☐	☐	50. The words *trainer* and *facilitator* have the same meaning.

Agree	Disagree	
☐	☐	51. In-house training programs are more effective than e-learning training programs.
☐	☐	52. Instructor-led programs are more effective than e-learning training programs.
☐	☐	53. The best approach to training participants is blended learning, which combines e-learning with instructor-led programs.
☐	☐	54. Trainers should conduct a workshop for managers on how to conduct productive meetings.
☐	☐	55. If trainers don't initiate it, managers should ask trainers to conduct a workshop on how to conduct productive meetings.

Answers to Pretest and Posttest

NOTE: Many of the answers that are "D" are because the statement is "not necessarily agree." This applies to all of the first six items and many others.

1.	D	20.	D	39.	D
2.	D	21.	A	40.	D
3.	D	22.	D	41.	A
4.	D	23.	D	42.	D
5.	D	24.	D	43.	D
6.	D	25.	A	44.	D
7.	A	26.	D	45.	A
8.	D	27.	A	46.	A
9.	D	28.	D	47.	A
10.	A	29.	D	48.	D
11.	A	30.	A	49.	D
12.	A	31.	A	50.	D
13.	A	32.	A	51.	D
14.	D	33.	A	52.	D
15.	D	34.	A	53.	D
16.	A	35.	A	54.	A
17.	A	36.	A	55.	A
18.	A	37.	A		
19.	A	38.	A		

NOTE: Score both your Pretest and Posttest and compare the scores. See what you learned and what concepts were confirmed. I would appreciate your Pretest and Posttest scores and any comments about the book. You may email them to dleekirk1@aol.com.

A Final Word

To Trainers:

There are two reasons why this book will be of benefit to you. First, it gives practical help for running instructor-led training courses. Second, it provides practical ideas for teaching a workshop for managers on how to conduct productive meetings. And I advise you to do it. When you read how much time is wasted in meetings and the costs of nonproductive meetings, you will see the need. Be sure to include a section on problem-solving meetings. And use case studies and role playing to make it interesting and enjoyable. If you wish to develop a lesson plan and check with me on content and approach, I will be happy to answer an email sent to dleekirk1@aol.com. I have conducted many such meetings and found them to be helpful to managers who conduct departmental and staff meetings.

To Managers:

You will find some practical ideas for conducting productive departmental and staff meetings. Chapter 11 was written especially for you. It is a practical approach to help you make quality decisions and get acceptance from those who must implement the solutions to your problems. Other chapters will also be helpful.

Let me urge you to ask your training professionals to conduct for you a workshop on how to conduct productive meetings. This will help you improve your departmental and staff meetings. In the typical departmental meeting, almost half of the time is considered wasted by the subordinates. And they go away from the meeting with bad attitudes toward the meeting and perhaps even toward the manager for conducting a nonproductive meeting. Don't let this happen to you!

Don Kirkpatrick

Appendix A

Practical Tips from Experienced Meeting Leaders

―――――――――――――――――――――――――――――――――――――――➤

Donald Kirkpatrick conducted a survey to obtain practical tips on how to conduct productive meetings.

Selection of Survey Participants

The survey was sent to meeting leaders who attended a workshop on how to conduct productive meetings. Three groups were included in the survey:

1. participants from various organizations who attended a one-day workshop conducted by Donald Kirkpatrick at the Management Institute of the University of Wisconsin-Milwaukee
2. selected meeting leaders at The Upjohn Company in Kalamazoo, Michigan, who attended a one-day workshop conducted by Donald Kirkpatrick
3. selected meeting leaders from the Information Systems and Management Sciences Department of Standard Oil Company of Indiana in Chicago who attended a two-day workshop conducted by Donald Kirkpatrick.

Number of Responses

Responses were received from 45 people, 21 of whom attended the University of Wisconsin-Milwaukee program, four from Upjohn, and 20 from Standard Oil of Indiana.

Kinds of Meetings They Conduct and Attend

The 45 people who completed the questionnaire conduct and attend meetings as shown in table A-1 and explained in further detail in table A-1-1 and table A-1-2.

Table A-1. Type and Frequency of Meetings.

	Conducted			Attended		
Type of Meeting	Departmental (Staff)	Instructional (Training)	Other	Departmental (Staff)	Instructional (Training)	Other
No. of Survey Participants	25	23	32	42	30	29
No. of Meetings per year	785	224	590	958	151	728

Table A-1-1. Survey Responses—Meetings You Conduct.

1. What are the three most significant factors that make your meetings productive (i.e., accomplish objectives in minimum time with satisfied participants)?

Response	Number of People Who Gave This Response
Preparation of agenda and objectives by leader	31
Control of the meeting by leader	17
Participation by members of group	14
Proper notice to participants and appropriate preparation by participants	14
Proper conclusion of meeting	12
Effective use of visual aids and handouts	7
Right participants in the meeting	7
Starting the meetings on time	6
Clear communication of objectives by leader	6
Knowledgeable and enthusiastic leader	3
Follow-up summary prepared and distributed	2
Appropriate facilities	1

2. What are the three most common factors that make your meetings nonproductive?

Response	Number of People Who Gave This Response
Lack of control by leader	34
Lack of preparation by participants	12
Lack of preparation by leader	11
Objectives and topic not clearly communicated by leader	9
Poor attitude of participants (lack of interest, etc.)	6
Wrong participants	6
Interruptions	5

Table A-1-1. Survey Responses—Meetings You Conduct (continued).

2. What are the three most common factors that make your meetings nonproductive? (continued)

Response	Number of People Who Gave This Response
Meeting wasn't necessary	4
Meeting held at a bad time	4
Tardiness of participants	4
Poor physical facilities	3
Lack of conclusion	1
Too much material to cover	1

3. What is your number one problem in conducting meetings?

Response	Number of People Who Gave This Response
Controlling the meeting	18
Maintaining interest and enthusiasm	7
Getting group members to participate	4
Getting started on time	3
Participants aren't prepared	3
When to hold the meeting	3
Better communication among leaders and participants	1

Table A-1-2. Survey Responses—Meetings You Attend.

1. What are the three most significant factors that make these meetings productive?

Response	Number of People Who Gave This Response
Control by leader	14
Participation by group	12
Preparation by leader	10
Objectives and agenda clear to participants	7
Proper advance notice to participants	5
Proper conclusion of meeting	5
Participants are well prepared	4
Right climate	3
Right place	3
Good communication between leader and group	3
Good audiovisual aids	2

(continued on page 106)

Table A-1-2. Survey Responses—Meetings You Attend (continued).

1. What are the three most significant factors that make these meetings productive? (continued)

Response	Number of People Who Gave This Response
On schedule	2
Right time	2
Right people	2
Meeting is short	1
Meeting is necessary	1
Appropriate breaks	1
Knowledgeable leader	1

2. What are the three most common factors that make these meetings nonproductive?

Response	Number of People Who Gave This Response
Lack of control by leader	23
Lack of preparation by leader	19
Poor (or no) conclusion	9
Meeting too long	9
Uninformed or unprepared participants	7
Wrong people	5
Too much material to cover	4
Leader is a poor communicator	4
Meeting was unnecessary	3
Lack of group interest	3
Lack of participation by group	3
Poor physical facilities	3
Outside interruptions	3
Not enough breaks	2
Poor audiovisual aids	2
Close-minded leader	1
Too much technical data	1
Lack of knowledge of group by leader	1
Didn't start on time	1

Best Suggestions

Here are some responses to the question, "What is the best suggestion you can give to people who conduct meetings?"

Standard Oil Company

"The importance of control of any conference without suppressing or inhibiting fruitful thought from its participants."

"Meetings should be like a good Chinese dinner: easily and happily consumed, readily digestible, and not too filling."

"Call the individuals the day of the meeting. Tell them you are starting sharply at _____, and you need them to be there. Will they be there?"

"Provide an agenda and sufficient advance notice to allow for preparation for the meeting."

"Be well prepared, and distribute an agenda prior to the start of the meeting. Start the meeting promptly and continue on, taking time only to resolve a point or defer it until later if a solution is not apparent."

"Prepare sufficiently before the meeting."

"Be completely prepared."

"Know what you want accomplished from the meeting, and plan your agenda to meet this goal."

"Plan meetings; get feedback; use eye contact."

Upjohn

"Consider the participants—who, when, where, and why."

"Tell them what you are going to tell them (brief) before you tell them (detail)."

"Set goals; sum up as often as necessary, especially if the group becomes repetitive or common agreement is not attained, and accomplish goals set up. If a decision is not reached and a committee is needed or additional information is needed, set up the next meeting or assign a person to write a memo to participants in a specified time."

"Always be sure that the people you invite to a meeting have a reason for being there. Do not invite people you think might just be interested."

Other Participants

"State purpose clearly, and check for feedback to see if participants understand."
—A nonprofit organization

"Cover all items on agenda; stick to it, but be flexible enough to allow discussion on items. Try to start meeting on time and finish on time."—A hospital

"Plan the meeting; communicate before and after; keep meetings on track."
—An insurance company

"Know your audience and their interests."—A manufacturer of electrical equipment

"Plan and prepare your meetings. Remember, you can't build a house without a blueprint."—A department store chain

"Be prepared; in fact, be overprepared."—A housewares company

"Know when a meeting is desirable, what has to be accomplished; were the objectives met with minimum amount of time, and were the participants happy with the conclusion?"—A restoration group

"Plan the meeting; follow the plan, but be flexible. Know the kind and purpose of the meeting, and conduct it accordingly."—A technical institute

"Be concise—concerned with the valuable time of others involved. Preplan, and prepare for the session. Stick to the plan—know when you are through (approximately)."—A hospital

"Write down the objective. Then ask oneself, 'Is a meeting necessary?' If yes, plan it properly, including who should be there."—A publishing company

"Know your participants, and be prepared."—A municipal government

"State clearly the true purpose of the meeting. Avoid hidden agendas. Be selective in choosing participants."—A municipal government

"Be organized."—A county public welfare department

"Learn as much about people as possible: why they attend meetings, why they behave as they do, why they can or cannot relate to each other, what motivates them, and what stimulates their thinking or action."—A university

"Know what you want to do; then think straight and talk straight!"—A university

"Be prompt; be concise; be fair, and listen."—A university

Appendix B

After the Meeting, What Then?

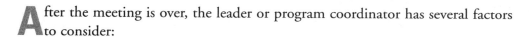

Aﬀer the meeting is over, the leader or program coordinator has several factors to consider:

- Will there be future meetings to conduct? How can I do better?
- Should I prepare and distribute a summary of the meeting? To whom?
- What follow-up is necessary?

Planning Future Meetings

In chapter 12, all meeting leaders are encouraged to evaluate a meeting immediately after it's over. The leader can use any combination of the three sources for evaluation: self-evaluation by the leader, reactions from the participants, and reactions from a trained observer. The purpose of this postmeeting evaluation is to obtain suggestions for improving future meetings and begin to plan for better meetings in the future.

Sometimes the meeting problems should be called to the attention of the right people. For example, if visual aids were not working properly, the problem should be called to the attention of the audiovisual person and the problem corrected. If the meeting room was not properly prepared, this should be called to the attention of the person responsible so it doesn't happen again. If the temperature was too hot or too cold, this fact should be communicated to the proper person so that future meetings will be held under ideal temperature conditions.

Summarizing the Meeting

The leader should consider whether a written summary is desirable. In fact, the decision should probably be made before the meeting is held. Either the leader or a designated secretary can take appropriate notes during the meeting to be used as the basis for the summary. If a secretary prepares the summary, it should be checked by the leader before reproduction and distribution.

A summary should be prepared and distributed if

- The people who attend the meeting want a summary either for their files or for clarification of what happened.
- The people who did not attend want to know what happened.
- The leader wants the participants to have a summary—perhaps decisions were reached and assignments given.
- The leader wants to communicate to those who didn't attend.
- The leader wants a written record of what happened.

"The horror of that moment," the king went on, "I shall never, never forget!"
"You will though," the queen said, "if you don't make a memorandum of it."

The queen was probably right. The king will forget unless he writes it down on paper.

This quote was taken from perhaps the most famous book on communication in the English language, Lewis Carroll's *Alice's Adventures in Wonderland*. The situation is a telling comment on something that frequently happens after a meeting. Ideas are not put on paper and, thus, are lost or forgotten. Therefore, follow-up summaries are important.

The length of the summary depends on the amount of detail that is wanted or needed by those who attended. In general, it should be a relatively brief description of objectives, accomplishments, and assignments. Sometimes, supplementary materials can be added.

Table B-1 shows a suggested format for a follow-up summary.

Following Up the Meeting

If decisions were reached on action to be taken, the leader should follow up to see that the appropriate action is taken. If assignments are given in the meeting, the leader should confirm these in writing to the persons involved. Also, the leader must follow up to see that the assignments are done.

Table B-1. Follow-up Summary Sheet.

From: (name of leader or coordinator)

To: (names of participants and others who should receive the summary listed alphabetically
            by last name)

Date:

Subject: (meeting topic)

Date of meeting: Times: (starting and ending)

Location:

In attendance: (listed alphabetically by last name)

Meeting objectives:

    1.

    2.

    3.

Accomplishments:

Assignments:

Additional comments:

Date of next meeting: Time: Place:

Appendix C

How to Contribute as a Participant

Most people who conduct meetings also attend meetings. The more skillful they become in conducting meetings, the more critical they become of the meetings they attend. So, how should people react when they are asked to attend a meeting they expect to be nonproductive? Several alternatives are available:

- Don't go. Make up a good excuse.
- Go, but demonstrate your dissatisfaction by refusing to participate, criticizing the leader, arguing, or exhibiting other nonproductive behavior.
- Go, and help the meeting be productive.

Obviously, the third alternative is usually the best. The problem is, how can a participant be helpful without causing resentment on the part of the leader? If the leader happens to be your boss, tact may be essential.

Here are some ways in which a participant can help a meeting become productive.

Know Why You Are There

If you don't get adequate notice, ask for it. Try to get details on time, place, and objectives so that you can plan and prepare to be there. Suggest that other participants get the same information.

Be There on Time

Get to the meeting before it is scheduled to begin. Be in your seat, ready to go. Encourage the leader to begin the meeting on time. You might tactfully say, "Well it's 9:00. Let's go." Or, "If you aren't going to start the meeting on time, I guess

I'll go back to my office to make a quick phone call." Hints like this will usually stimulate the leader to start on time.

Stay on the Subject

Be sure you know the subject being discussed and the objectives of the meeting. If you participate, stay on the subject. If you aren't sure what the subject is, ask for clarification—not only for your own benefit but also for the benefit of the group. You could say, "Will you put the objective (or question) on the board (flipchart) so it's clear to all of us?"

Don't Cause Problems for the Leader

Go to the meeting with a positive attitude and an objective to help make the meeting be as productive as possible. Here are a few things to remember:

- Don't start side conversations. Ignore anyone who tries to start a side conversation with you.
- Don't be interrupted by a telephone message unless it's an emergency.
- Don't argue with the leader or with another member of the group. Challenge, yes, but avoid arguments.
- Don't lose control of your emotions.
- Don't hesitate to ask questions if you aren't sure about something.
- Don't try to do other work during the meeting.

Be Open to the Ideas of Others

It's amazing how open-mindedness begets open-mindedness. When you are willing to listen and are open-minded to the ideas of others, they are more apt to be open-minded toward the ideas you present. When responding to their ideas, use such comments as:

- "I see what you mean."
- "I understand how you feel."
- "You have a good point there."
- "I hadn't thought of it that way."

Help the Leader Control the Meeting

Be on the alert for the meeting getting out of control. When it does, respond in one of the following ways:

- If heated arguments occur between participants, put yourself in between. See if you can help each one see the other person's side.

- If one participant dominates, inject your own ideas or ask for a contribution from another person by saying, "I'd like to hear Bill's ideas on the subject."
- If interruptions or distractions occur, say, "I wonder if we can get back to our objective."
- If you feel that a participant is off the subject, gently bring the conversation back on track with a comment like, "I'm not sure how this ties in with the objective." This might stimulate the leader to restate the objective or the question being discussed.
- If the meeting gets out of control, try to bring it back by restating the objective and summarizing what has been accomplished and what needs to be done.

Use a Problem-Solving Method

Here is a summary of four participant opportunities in a problem-solving conference:

1. Contribute ideas to the discussion.
   - Understand why you are attending the meeting.
   - Make sure you understand the problem.
   - Offer facts and opinions where appropriate.
   - Maintain dissenting views in the fact of opposition but not to the point of having a closed mind or being obnoxious.

2. Listen to the ideas of others.
   - Listen carefully.
   - Understand the viewpoints of others.
   - Help others to develop their views and ideas.
   - Be courteous by respecting other opinions even if they are different from your own.

3. Consider the problem objectively.
   - Maintain an objective attitude.
   - Avoid giving or accepting opinions as facts.
   - Avoid becoming emotional.

4. Contribute to the orderly conduct of the meeting.
   - Arrange matters so that personal interruptions are unnecessary.
   - Be prompt.
   - Avoid side conversations with neighbors.
   - Stay on the subject.

- Refrain from dominating the meeting.
- Help the leader maintain order.

Pay Attention

You won't be able to contribute at all unless you are attentive. Perhaps the first words of advice are *pay attention*! Sometimes this is very difficult to do because the subject is dry, the leader is a poor communicator, the physical facilities are poor, or you have something on your mind that bothers you. You, therefore, are tempted to become a poor listener.

Below are five ways to stay attentive and listen even if you are bored or distracted.

1. *Find areas of interest.* Look for ideas and topics that can be useful to you. These ideas can come from the leader or other participants.
2. *Judge content, not delivery.* Don't be upset and distracted by a monotone voice or the fact that the speaker is reading the material.
3. *Hold your fire.* Don't get overstimulated and sent off on an emotional tangent because of a word or phrase that the speaker used.
4. *Resist distractions.* Sometimes it's easy to remove distractions by closing a door, turning off a fan, or pulling a window shade. Sometimes it requires concentration.
5. *Take notes.* In addition to the mental process to improve attentiveness and listening, the physical process of taking notes can be helpful. A person who takes notes during a meeting is more able to resist boredom and disinterest than one who doesn't. Obviously, note taking requires listening, and a person who vows to come out of a meeting with notes is committed to listening.

A Note-Taking Technique

The note taker simply records the main words or ideas in the same order that the speaker presents them. If the speaker says, "My first point is...," the note taker labels it "1." The note taker tries to put these points down in the same order and with the same emphasis as the speaker. If the speaker says, "I want to emphasize the next point," the note taker puts down an asterisk, underlines it, or labels it "significant." Without worrying about a formal outline, or facts versus principles, the note taker exerts self-discipline to listen and take notes. Perhaps the notes will be referred to again and perhaps not. But the note-taking process has served one important purpose—to force the listener to listen. Also, the very process of writing will improve the retention of the listener, whether or not the notes are reviewed at a later date.

The participant is an important ingredient of a productive meeting. The first requirement is to pay attention to what is being said. In addition, there are many things a participant can do to help make the meeting productive:

- Know why you are there.
- Be there on time.
- Stay on the subject.
- Don't cause problems for the leader.
- Be open to the ideas of others.
- Help the leader control the meeting.
- Use a problem-solving method.
- Pay attention.

What Is Your Profile as a Meeting Participant?

Good meeting participants:

1. Plan for the meeting.
   - Think about the problem ahead of time.
   - Talk with others who know something about the problem.
   - Get as many facts as time allows.
   - Understand why they are attending.

2. Contribute ideas to the discussion .
   - Offer facts and ideas.
   - Don't quickly discard views in the face of opposition.
   - Understand the facts.
   - Understand the problem.

3. Listen to the ideas of others.
   - Understand the viewpoints of others.
   - Help others develop their views and ideas.
   - Be courteous and alert.
   - Listen carefully and think.

4. Consider the problem objectively.
   - Maintain an objective attitude.
   - Avoid giving (or accepting) opinions as fact.
   - Avoid emotionalism.
   - Maintain confidences and avoid gossip.

5. Contribute to the orderly conduct of the meeting.
   - Arrive on time.
   - Help the leader maintain order.
   - Make arrangements to avoid personal interruptions.
   - Avoid side conversations.
   - Do not dominate the meeting.
   - Stay on the subject.
   - Avoid sarcasm and ridicule.

Appendix D

Do's and Don'ts for Conducting Meetings

➤

The joys and sorrows, successes and failures of meetings past are reflected in these do's and don'ts of planning and conducting such meetings. Born of experience, the do's and don'ts below are those of 50 or more sales promotion managers, marketing executives, and others expert in their companies' meetings, who listed their suggestions at the request of *Advertising Age*. They apply especially to large sales conferences.

Do's

Preparing the Meeting, Do...

1. Choose a theme, and plan around it.
2. Have a motivation theme tied to objectives, mentality, and accomplishments.
3. Plan and schedule events; hold to the schedule.
4. Have detailed plans for every hour of the meeting.
5. Prepare a checklist of every detail for every day.
6. Plan enough in advance to have materials on hand.
7. Develop a master checklist.
8. Program carefully. On three- or four-day meetings, give a half-day off to enjoy the local scene.
9. Have a dry run of the meeting before the scheduled time.
10. Screen individual presentations carefully; edit for maximum effect.
11. Insist on use of visuals by everyone. Any speaker who will not take time to prepare applicable visuals doesn't deserve the privilege of appearing on your program.

12. Make sure each presenter has the appropriate attitude.

13. Make every presentation to the point; don't ramble.

14. Be well prepared. A good speaker should be able to cover every possible important point in one hour.

15. Force an outline form and, if possible, a rehearsal by each presenter.

Preparing for the Meeting, Do...

1. Permit ample time for individual, regional, or district meetings so that territorial problems do not have to be discussed or take up the time of the meeting itself.

2. Have district managers meet prior to the regular meeting so that you know you are working on the correct problems.

3. Visit the site for an on-the-spot inspection prior to the meeting.

4. Check the facilities for problems, such as lighting and sound capabilities.

5. Make sure preparations are complete and detailed.

6. Triple check air circulation and heating and cooling facilities.

7. Have the meeting room properly set up, not only to show the theme, but also to indicate the meeting is well conceived and not just thrown together at the last moment.

Preparing the Participants for the Meeting, Do...

1. Provide ample notice to participants.

2. Issue in advance a program schedule and topics.

3. Give plenty of advance notice as to the date and place of meeting.

4. Have advance registrations and name badges ready.

5. Try to precondition attendees by use of a good slogan. Then tie in your bulletins, memos, or house publications with this theme or slogan.

6. Make sure everyone has an outline for the meeting before it begins.

7. Get everyone to be a part of the meeting by publishing a questionnaire beforehand, asking for complaints. Go through these and make a decision at the meeting regarding what your company policy is or will be.

Remembering Key Points of the Meeting, Do...

1. Start on time; stay on time; end on time.

2. Use early-bird prizes to get sessions started on time; then police the speakers to stay within time limits.

3. Open with a bang, not a sour note that spells defeat or discouragement.

4. Have the company president address the participants and attend the opening meeting.
5. End the meeting on a high note.
6. Leave the participants with an immediate action program and realistic objectives.
7. Leave time between the end of the meeting and flight departures.

During the Meeting, Do...

1. Take time to listen; encourage discussion.
2. Take a positive stand.
3. Keep the agenda loose enough to allow free time.
4. Promote discussion topics in advance, and allow each person time to give opinions.
5. Keep meetings lively, brief.
6. Use a little showmanship.
7. Keep the meeting moving on a predetermined schedule.
8. Discuss only positive information that is geared to ignite enthusiasm at general meeting sessions.
9. Give it your all; if an event is worth doing, it is worth doing well.
10. Vary for interest.
11. Use gimmicks for laughs to relax listeners.
12. Use visuals—slides, movies, and so forth—and keep them short. Change these daily.
13. Use meeting prizes; they are effective and helpful.
14. Light the meeting room well.
15. Vary the speakers.
16. Make presentations short.
17. Provide time for question-and-answer sessions.
18. Provide adequate entertainment.
19. Carry doubles of all films and slides.
20. Break into shirtsleeve sessions for detailed discussion on the program presented—moderated by the home-office team plus other people thoroughly briefed on the program.
21. Involve participants as much as possible.
22. Involve key agency personnel in the live presentation; it's wonderful exposure for them.
23. Use plenty of room decorations relating to the program.

24. Review corporate progress, particularly in a multidivisional company, and state clearly the divisional objectives.

25. Maintain a fast-moving, variegated program with adequate time for two-way discussion.

26. Recognize good performance.

27. Show how the department fits into the overall plans of the corporation.

28. Keep the department aware of corporate goals.

29. Stress importance of communications.

30. Include people from other departments in the meeting.

31. Provide an interesting, but businesslike, meeting.

32. Call on outside professional assistance for either the entire production or the specific responsibilities of production.

33. Start fast and end fast—with dramatics at both ends.

34. Have an element of surprise.

35. Build the meeting so you can have a series of small climaxes, culminated with the prime climax—banquet and awards.

36. Get problem solving done early in the meeting—via workshops or buzz sessions.

37. Change the pace of the meeting every day; insist on program variety.

38. Allow time for recreation.

39. Keep the meeting purpose and objectives clear in everyone's mind.

40. Insist on elbow room, but avoid the ballroom atmosphere. It should be cozy enough for a friendly feeling, but room enough for comfort.

41. Keep sessions short—30 minutes if you can. If longer, break up into segments.

42. Use as much audiovisual equipment as possible. Check and recheck all equipment after it is set up in the meeting room. Nothing kills a meeting like a public address system or a projector that won't work. Rehearse presentations with the equipment operator when using films or slides.

43. Make awards sessions in the form of dinner meetings with spouses and company personnel in attendance. Recognition should be as public as possible.

44. Enforce the wearing of name tags—by everyone.

45. Use natural enthusiasm, not artificial props.

46. Use goals, but stimulate thought on how goals may be obtained.

47. Carry away the synopsis of the meeting.

48. Lend interest through well-done skits.

49. Use imagination and showmanship to make points.

During Down Time, Do...

1. Bring in outside experts for luncheon or dinner speakers.
2. Assign members of the top management team to certain tables so they can mix with others at meal functions. The formality of a head table is out. This builds for a closer relationship and understanding of management and field personnel.
3. Have off periods where attendees can relax, socialize, and so forth.
4. Keep noon lunches light.
5. Give the participants accessories, like desk organizers, pads, briefcases, and so forth.

Meeting with Fellow Presenters, Do...
1. Hold briefings with work crew daily to outline jobs to be done during the next 24 hours.
2. Make one person responsible for the whole show with others responsible for specific jobs. Let the hotel understand that this person is to be the leader and only that person is to give orders.

After the Meeting, Do...
1. Postmortem a meeting series immediately upon conclusion.
2. Arrange a field follow-up.
3. Serve coffee and refreshments.

Don'ts
Preparing for the Meeting, Don't...
1. Cut costs by eliminating the little things.
2. Try to pack too much into a program. It is better to go to an extra day or to have early evening sessions.
3. Count on the hotel to have the technical help you need—electricians, stagehands, audiovisual-sound systems, and so forth. Contact outside experts.
4. Overdo evening pre-meeting hospitality.
5. Pinch pennies in selecting the site or running the meeting. If it's worth hauling the participants in from all over, it's worth giving them the feeling that the company cares enough to treat them in a first-class manner.
6. Permit pre-meeting cocktail parties that leave the audience beat and with dulled senses.
7. Use a drastic new idea without first checking it out.
8. Hold a meeting at a new place without checking its references, and then checking the actual facilities.

During the Meeting, Don't...

1. Dwell on the dull figures, quotas, and so forth.
2. Review individual account activity in the presence of the entire meeting.
3. Allow gripe sessions to develop.
4. Drag out executive speeches.
5. Just talk about what's wrong.
6. Get monotonous. Have key personnel discuss various facets, programs, or policies.
7. Be too cute. Hold entertainment and humor for off-duty hours.
8. Use all the time for talking at the people.
9. Use too much ham. You are likely to get eggs for results.
10. Use the same format each year. Keep it fresh.
11. Use too many visuals. Alternate it or run it concurrently with live action.
12. Undercut your own people by giving orders to hotel staff in areas in which you have no responsibility.
13. Forget that you are helping to stage the convention.
14. Use photographic slides crowded with copy that can't be read easily and will not be remembered.
15. Present extraneous subjects that stray from the theme of the meeting.
16. Bore the participants.
17. Single anyone out for criticism.
18. Challenge the participants to beat a quota.
19. Keep the participants sitting in one place for too long.
20. Let one person dominate the whole show. Meetings seem to be a great place for self-styled leaders to preach endlessly.
21. Allow dull, monotonous talks that are read meticulously from scripts.
22. Let any speaker keep slides on the screen interminably.
23. Fall into such a standard format that the participants know what is coming.
24. Invite management to speak without suggesting ground rules concerning the subject and amount of time.
25. Schedule one heavy or technical subject after another without interspersing lighter presentations or participating sessions.
26. Allow the character of the recreational program to override the importance of the meeting.
27. Use boring statistics.
28. Get too elementary. Keep it sophisticated.

29. Bore the pros.
30. Discuss, in general sessions, subjects that are of interest to only a portion of the group. Allow time for special interest sessions.

During Down Time, Don't...
1. Overfeed the participants.
2. Put undue stress on the gimmicks, showmanship, and so forth, that might get in the way of the guts of what the participants wish to hear about.
3. Forget to outline the action you expect as a result of the meeting.

Appendix E

Murphy's Law
at Meetings

Murphy's Law states simply that if anything can go wrong, it will. From experience, many would add, of those things that can't possibly go wrong, most will.

Some conference planners go through a "What if..." exercise, imagining all of the dire possibilities. Many expect that Murphy's Law would operate in this effort also: The most potentially devastating occurrence will not be foreseen.

Nevertheless, there really should be a way to help meeting planners and facility staffs more systematically examine the potentials for failure if only to narrow down the event that will remain unforeseen. Following is an aid based on Allen Zoll's (1975) "Reverse Check List for Meeting Planners: What If Any of These 68 Meeting Details Go Awry?" to help meeting planners in such an activity.

I. Site Selection and Arrangements

I:1   Once the hotel and you are committed for dates and rooms, a 3,000-person patriotic convention with marching bands will be booked also. Then maintenance, construction, and painting can be scheduled.

I:2   Stated hotel meeting room capacities will be based on actual usage by Marine Corps drill instructors. For other uses, divide by three.

I:3   Rooms inspected in advance will diminish in size by one-half between selection and use.

I:4   A request for a U-shape table arrangement will be modified to a W-shape to take into account the large columns that have suddenly appeared.

I:5   Divisible large rooms with guaranteed soundproof partitions will be none of these.

I:6   The phrase "comfortable, stackable chairs" will be contradictory. Metal folding chairs will appear.

I:7   When all advance preparations have been worked out perfectly, sleeping rooms will be overbooked.

I:8   Priorities assigned in the final booking of rooms will vary inversely with the length of time arrangements were made ahead.

II. Materials

II:1   Materials essential for preconference preparation will not be received by participants. When received, the materials will not be read.

II:2   Materials shipped ahead to yourself at the hotel will be returned since you are not registered.

II:3   When inadvertently kept, advance materials may be stored in the pastry pantry of the annex kitchen. You will know for sure when the person with the key arrives at work the day of the conference start.

II:4   Materials taken as baggage for safekeeping will be transshipped.

II:5   In transit, prepunched holes will heal, clear printing will fade, collated materials will regroup, and felt pens will cast off their tops.

II:6   Handouts will be 10 percent short.

II:7   Pages four and five of the key handout will be missing.

III. Prearrangements

III:1 Meeting rooms with seating, name cards, handouts, and displays arranged the night before will disappear.

III:2 There will be an inverse relation between the popularity of a concurrent meeting and the size of the room scheduled for it.

III:3 In any random seating arrangement, the highest status persons present will be seated at the table legs.

III:4 After subgroups have been formed and pretyped, persons named Clair, Pat, Ollie, Leslie, Jean, Marion, and Will will be the opposite gender from whatever you assumed.

IV. Program Scheduling

IV:1 The necessity for program changes will increase as the date approaches. The final surge will coincide with the printed program delivery.

IV:2 All five-minute business meetings called between functions will last 40 minutes.

IV:3 Restarting the program after breaks will be delayed from 10 to 30 minutes without bulldozers.

V. Communications

V:1 Letters left at the front desk for participants to receive at Sunday check-in will be placed in mailboxes on the following Thursday.

V:2 The meeting schedule, when posted at all in the lobby, will be correct within one hour of the starting and ending times. Organizational abbreviations will be creative.

V:3 Three groups with similar names will be booked with your conference. This assures that one-third of your group will be elsewhere and one-third of those present should be elsewhere.

V:4 As soon as the front desk, the assistant manager, the catering office, and the bell captain all clearly understand your urgent needs, the shift will change.

VI. Ventilation and Temperature

VI:1 Ventilation and temperature controls will be part of the room décor and not meant to be functional.

VI:2 The ventilation system capability will vary inversely to the number of smokers multiplied by the number of militant nonsmokers.

VI:3   The mean temperature of meeting rooms will be ideal. The range will present constant problems.

VII. Guest Speakers

VII:1   The more simple a switch in speakers appears, the further its complications will extend.

VII:2   Speakers with *horse* topics will have to be shifted to later in the program; those with *cart* topics will be glad to be scheduled earlier.

VII:3   A reasonable number of speakers will report to the chain's other hotel across town.

VII:4   The bar will generally be popular as the site for final preparation by the speakers.

VII:5   The substitute for the keynote speaker will send a substitute. His profuse apologies will highlight his presentation.

VII:6   Two of your speakers will bring a talk prepared for another occasion. One will present his anyway; the other will speak extempore for an hour.

VII:7   Three of the speakers will use the same involved humorous anecdote to begin their talks. The varying degrees of off-colorness will be only mildly interesting.

VII:8   The availability of copy service will be inverse to the speaker's need for it.

VII:9   If there are X places set at the head table, X plus three important people will arrive to sit there.

VII:10 The occasions when two people arise to introduce the speaker will be balanced by the occasions when no one does.

VIII. Refreshments and Meals

VIII:1 Refreshments will arrive at a critical point in the speaker's talk or just before or after lunch.

VIII:2 Coffee service will be incorrect by a factor of two or one-half; bills for service will reflect the higher error factor.

VIII:3 Refreshments arriving on time and containing the correct mixture of coffee, tea, and soft drinks will have been sent to your sleeping room.

VIII:4   For religious or dietary reasons, or for reasons of custom, cottage cheese and lettuce will be the only universally unrestricted food. One-half of the group will not be able to abide cottage cheese.

VIII:5   One-half of the group will mention that there is not enough food. The other half will observe that there is too much. All will complain that they are gaining weight.

VIII:6   Table seating arrangements for meals will not take into account that shoulder width tends to be broader than width at the knees for seated persons.

VIII:7   Meal functions at round tables further immediate, involved discussion. They are always two butter plates and salads short.

VIII:8   Some will not be finished with dessert when it's time to begin the after-dinner program. But some will not have been served the entrée, either.

VIII:9   The postmeal activity of the serving staff will provide an interesting alternative for those not captivated by the planned programs.

IX. Audiovisual

IX:1   The PA system in use in adjoining rooms will be piped into your meeting room as a convenience.

IX:2   Room lighting controls will be found in the pantry behind the kitchen.

IX:3   The light switches will also control the outlet where the audiovisual equipment is plugged in.

IX:4   Wall outlets will lack the third hole for the grounding pin for all audiovisual equipment. The bellperson, sent for adapters or wire cutters, will report on return that the hardware store is closed.

IX:5   Electrical cords not taped down to floors will add interest (and sometimes a few laughs) to sessions.

IX:6   Extension cords will be two and one-half feet too short.

IX:7   Borrowed audiovisual equipment will add interest because of their intrinsic value as collector's items.

IX:8   Spare bulbs for audiovisual equipment will malfunction.

IX:9   The projector lens focal length will be in inverse relation to the length of the room.

IX:10   The ideal location for the screen will be just under the one light remaining on when the room is darkened.

IX:11   Visual aids used in the hotel's *mirror room* will provide psychedelic effects.

IX:12   Films received at the last minute before showing will not have been rewound.

IX:13   A film that has been correctly cleaned, inspected, rewound, threaded, and introduced will break.

IX:14   Film cans clearly marked "Management Controls" will contain a film on spot welding. Somewhere in circulation is a vice-versa set.

IX:15   Take-up reels will be two-thirds the size of the film reel.

IX:16   Bedspreads and sheets, when used as emergency projection screens, will produce an interesting effect—floral patterns even more so.

IX:17   Podiums will be the ideal height and focal distance for the average speaker. The average speaker will be unable to attend.

IX:18   The amplification system will fail during the talk of the least forceful speaker and be repaired during the talk of the most.

IX:19   Unstable flipchart legs and chalkboard stands will be conversation pieces.

IX:20   There will be no organizational connection at the hotel for suppliers of chalkboards, chalk, and erasers.

References

"191 Do's and Don'ts for Conducting Sales Meetings." *Advertising Age*, December 12, 1966.

Kirkpatrick, Donald L. *Evaluating Training Programs: The Four Levels* (3rd edition). San Francisco: Berrett-Koehler Publishers, 2006.

Kirkpatrick, Donald L. "Supervisory Inventory on Communication" Inventories. 1998. www.kirkpatrickfourlevels.com.

Odiorne, George. *The Change Resistors*. New York: Prentice-Hall, 1981.

Zoll, Allen. "Reverse Check List for Meeting Planners: What If Any of These 68 Meeting Details Go Awry?" *Successful Meetings*, October 1975.

About the Author

D onald L. Kirkpatrick is an active author, consultant, teacher, and speaker. He retired after more than 30 years with the Management Institute, University of Wisconsin where he planned and conducted meetings for all levels of management. He now holds the title of professor emeritus.

Kirkpatrick received three degrees from the University of Wisconsin in Madison: a BBA in accounting, an MBA in personnel management, and a PhD in counseling and adult education. His dissertation was on evaluating a human relations program for supervisors, where he developed his famous four levels for evaluating training programs.

His professional background includes positions as training manager with International Minerals and Chemical Corporation and human resources manager with Bendix Products Aerospace Division. He consulted for many organizations in the United States, including Blockbuster, Caterpillar, Ford, General Electric, IBM, PacifiCorp, United Nations, and World Bank. In foreign countries, he conducted programs in Argentina, Australia, Brazil, France, Greece, Hong Kong, India, Japan, Korea, Malaysia, Netherlands, Poland, Singapore, Spain, Taiwan, Thailand, Turkey, and Venezuela. He is a past national president and a Gordon M. Bliss award winner of the American Society for Training & Development. In 2004, he received ASTD's highest award, Lifetime Achievement in Workplace Learning and Performance. In 1997, he was elected to *Training* magazine's HRD Hall of Fame. He is a former national board member of the Society for Human Resources Management and a winner of a Research and two Best Book of the Year awards.

Kirkpatrick has written many articles and six books, including *No-Nonsense Communication* (1998), *Improving Employee Performance Through Appraisal and Coaching,* 2nd edition (2006), *Managing Change Effectively* (2002), *Developing Supervisors and Team Leaders* (2002), *Transferring Learning to Behavior* (coauthored with son, Jim) (2005), and *Evaluating Training Programs: The Four Levels,* 3rd edition (2006), which has been translated into Spanish, Polish, Turkish, and Chinese.

He has also written supervisory/management inventories on communication; human relations; time management; managing change; performance appraisal and coaching; and leadership, motivation, and decision making.

Kirkpatrick is a Gideon, senior elder at Elmbrook Church in Brookfield, Wisconsin, and chairman of the Board of South Asian Ministries, which supports a missionary in India. His hobbies include fishing, golfing, playing tennis, and watching the Wisconsin Badgers and Green Bay Packers.

He is married to Fern whom he met in the University of Wisconsin band. They have four children and five grandchildren.

Index